SPEAK

A Handbook for Effective Public Speaking

published by

ARTSCROLL

SHAAR PRESS

AVI SHULMAN

Illustrations by Shepsil Scheinberg

This book is respectfully dedicated to

Rabbi Moshe Sherer, zt"l

*who for more than five decades
was the spokesperson
for Torah ideals in America, Israel and worldwide.*

*He was a most eloquent speaker
who knew exactly how to motivate an audience,
how to inspire them to work for Klal Yisrael,
whether he was addressing a banquet,
an Agudath Israel convention,
a small group at his office,
thousands of youngsters at a rally,
or tens of thousands at a Siyum HaShas.*

*Rabbi Sherer fervently believed
that every ben Torah should speak effectively
and articulately to create a Kiddush Hashem.*

*His Public Speaking classes in Mesifta Torah Vodaath
were responsible for inspiring many young men
to become leaders in Agudath Israel,
in rabbonus and in chinuch.*

---

*Rabbi Sherer's Thirteen Key Points for effective public speaking
appear in chapter ten of this book.*

"**... ועשו סיג לתורה ...** יראה לי בביאור זה, שהוא הזהיר להיות כל אדם שומר פתחי פיו, בל יכביד השומעים בהם, וכל שכן כשמדבר בדברי תורה, שלא ידבר בהם אלא בזמן הראוי, בשיעור הראוי, במקום הראוי לו, ובדברים הראויים לו ..."

"Make a boundary for Torah..."

I believe the purpose of this passage is to caution every person to be careful with his speech, not to burden his listeners, especially when he presents Torah thoughts. He should speak only on the proper occasion, for the appropriate length of time, in the appropriate place and on subjects with which he is familiar.

Meiri (Ethics of the Fathers 1:1)

"דבש וחלב תחת לשונך"

"כל שאומר דברי תורה ברבים ואינם ערבים לשומעיהם כדבש וחלב המעורבים זה בזה, נוח לו שלא אמרן ..."

"Honey and milk under your tongue..." (Song of Songs, 4:11)

This verse teaches that if a person teaches Torah publicly and his words are not as sweet as milk and honey, it would be better that they had not been said. *Meiri commentary to Proverbs*

Advice of the Chofetz Chaim, zt"l

The Chofetz Chaim encouraged his students who aspired to be rabbis to learn to speak in public. He suggested they go to their empty *shul* on Friday afternoons, stand at the *bimah* and practice their speeches.

Preface

*M*ore than twenty-five years ago, I was urged by my colleagues in Torah Umesorah to teach kollel men how to communicate more effectively in public. As a result, I read many books on public speaking and interviewed people who teach this subject in universities, business schools and in personal growth programs.

The observant Jew who has learned even a few years in yeshivah has a wealth of insights into Torah, Talmud, ethics, Jewish history and Torah personalities. The challenge to the *ben Torah* or *bas Yisroel* (who has the opportunity and the ability to inspire other women) is how to select the most appropriate thoughts from this vast treasury of Jewish thought, how to prepare it and how to present it.

This book is an outgrowth of the courses I gave and continue to give at the Torah Umesorah Aish Dos Teacher Training Program, the Mercaz Teacher Training Program and various other public speaking programs. I am deeply grateful to the leadership of these organizations for the opportunities they afforded me. I also would like to express my appreciation to my son, Rabbi Yakov Yehuda Shulman, for his creativity in developing this program.

I would like to thank Rabbis Meir Zlotowitz and Nosson Scherman, both lifelong friends; Rabbi Sheah Brander; editor

Charlotte Friedland; Art Director Eli Kroen; graphics department staff members Tzini Hanover and Frady Vorhand; and illustrator Shepsil Scheinberg of Lakewood, New Jersey. We all owe the entire ArtScroll-Mesorah organization an enormous debt of gratitude because they have provided us with insights into *tefillah*, Tanach, Talmud, Jewish history and Jewish thought that have immeasurably enhanced learning opportunities for everyone.

In Appreciation

First, I wish to express profound gratitude to Hashem for having given me so much — life, health, talents, opportunities, a very special family, friends and community. I am especially blessed to have been always associated with *Roshei Yeshivah*, *Rabbonim*, *bnei Torah* and Torah personalities.

While I have received guidance and direction from many *Roshei Yeshivah*, and greatly benefited from my association with them, I would be remiss if I failed to express a special *hakoras hatov* to Rabbi Shmuel Kaminetsky, *shlita*, and to Rabbi Matisyahu Salomon, *shlita*, on whom I call very often.

The *yiras Shamayim*, integrity and dedication to Torah of my father, *zt"l*, are a constant inspiration to me. No doubt, the benevolence Hashem has given me is a result of *z'chus avos*.

I want to express appreciation to the very special people who over the last years have embraced me with concern, support and true friendship. Each in his own way, at the right time, has helped and encouraged me. In many ways, my venture into public speaking and the teaching of public speaking is a result of the confidence they had in me.

My heartfelt thanks go to my wife Erica, our children and their extended families, as well as to...

...A group of old friends who believed in me years ago: Dr. Joseph Kaminetsky, *zt"l*; Mr. And Mrs. Yale Gibber; Rabbi Gavriel Ginsberg; Rabbi Ben D. Eisenberg; Rabbi Moshe Goldberger; Mr. Yaakov Brecher; Rabbi Yisroel Flam and his rebbetzin, Noa Flam.

...My Torah Umesorah family, with special appreciation to Rabbi Joshua Fishman.

...My S.E.E.D. family, with special appreciation to Rabbi Joseph Grunfeld of London and all the kollel men and women who volunteered their time.

...My Mercaz family, with special appreciation to Rabbis Berel and Chaim Wein and Rabbi Joel Kramer.

...My Aish Dos family, with special appreciation to Rabbi Dovid Bernstein.

...My ArtScroll family, my Mesivta Bais Shraga family, my Yeshiva of Spring Valley family, my Daf Yomi family, my *rebbes* and *chavrusos*, all my good friends, and my "boys club." A special thank you to Rabbi Avrohom Greenfeld.

I am indebted to Rabbis Joshua Fishman, Jack Rachenbach and Pinchos Lipshutz for encouraging my writing of the Torah Umesorah articles and for sponsoring them in *Yated Ne'eman*.

Rabbis Paysach Krohn and Yissocher Frand have shown us how effective public speaking can be used to teach Torah and *yiras Shamayim* to the public. I so greatly appreciate their inspiration.

Avi Shulman
Cheshvan, 5762

About the Author

Avi Shulman was a classroom teacher for more than twenty-five years. He served as National Director of Torah Umesorah's S.E.E.D. program and currently teaches at the Aish Dos and Mercaz Teacher Training Programs.

He is the author of twenty personal growth and parenting books and cassette programs, and he writes a popular weekly column for Torah Umesorah published by *Yated Ne'eman*.

Mr. Shulman is a nationally acclaimed speaker and teacher.

Table of Contents

Do You Need a Quick Course in Public Speaking? Turn first to the HELP chapters! These chapters constitute a Quick Course that will equip you for your upcoming speaking engagement.

Chapter One

INTRODUCTION

- Can You Learn Public Speaking from a Book?   15
- How This Book Came to be Written   16
- Where Do We Go From Here?   18

Chapter Two

IT ALL STARTS WITH YOUR ATTITUDE

- The Born Public Speaker   21
- Yes, You Can   23
- Why Learn to Speak in Public?   23
- Excuses, and How to Override Them   26
- "I'm better When I'm Spontaneous"   30

Chapter Three

YOUR AUDIENCE

- Who is the Audience?   33

☍ Getting Answers to These Important Questions   36

▶   Are There Captive Audiences?   36

Chapter Four

SPEECH PREPARATION

▶   Food for the Mind   41

▶   When Do You Start to Prepare?   44

▶   When Pride Prevents Preparation   46

▶   Define Your Goals   48

    ▶ *What is the purpose of the speech?*
      Speeches to inform, to entertain, to persuade,
      to convince, to actuate, to impress

    ▶ *Where will I be speaking?*

    ▶ *How much time is allocated?*

    ▶ *What is the occasion?*

☍ The Mechanics of a Speech   54

    ▶ *Three Easy Steps*

☍ How to Organize a Speech   64

▶   Writing Vs. Speaking   68

▶   Time and the Jewish Problem   71

▶   Using an Audience Take-Home Sheet   74

☍ *WORKSHEETS — THE SPEECH ORGANIZER*

WORKSHEET A

▶   Developing Your Speech   77

WORKSHEET B
- ▶ Key Words   78
WORKSHEET C
- ▶ Audience Take-Home Sheet   78

Chapter Five

SPEECH COMPONENTS AND TECHNIQUES

- ▶ Telling a Story   79
- ▶ Humor   82
- ▶ Statistics   85
- ▶ The Torah Thought   86

Chapter Six

VERBAL AND NON-VERBAL MESSAGES

- ▶ Watch Your Words   91
- ▶ Keep It Simple   92
- ⊗ Six Messages We Want to Send to Our Audiences
     (Without Saying So)   95
- ▶ Podium: Friend or Foe?   101

Chapter Seven

TIPS ON PRESENTATION

- ▶ How to Dress for a Speech   105
- ▶ Just Before You Speak   107
- ▶ Overcoming Nervousness   109
- ▶ Don't Put Yourself Down   111
- ▶ We're Looking At You!   113

Chapter Eight

INTRODUCTIONS: HOW TO MAKE THEM AND HOW TO SURVIVE THEM

- ‣ When You Are the Chairman — 115
- ‣ How to Make an Introduction — 118
- ‣ Elements of the Introduction — 120
- ‣ How to Survive an Introduction — 123

Chapter Nine

IMPROVING YOUR SKILLS — 125
- ‣ Using a TAGI Sheet — 125
- Stimulating Your Ideas and Creative Thoughts — 130

Chapter Ten

YOU: THE PROFESSIONAL SPEAKER

- ‣ Take Control — 135
- ‣ Lights On — 139
- ‣ Using the Speaker's Information Questionnaire — 140
- ‣ Teaching Communication Skills to Children and Students — 144

Appendix A:

OPENINGS WITH A CHALLENGE — 149

Appendix B:

OPENINGS WITH A QUESTION — 151

Appendix C:

OPENINGS WITH A STATEMENT — 153

Chapter One
INTRODUCTION

*E*ffective public speaking does not begin when the speaker steps up to the podium. It springs from a bedrock foundation of self-esteem, self-discipline and creativity. It begins deep within and radiates outward to influence others positively.

Can You Learn Public Speaking from a Book?

That's a good question, and the answer is yes and no. If you expect to read a book and then magically stand up to expertly address a large audience, the answer is a resounding no! But if you are looking for ways to overcome your fears and learn the tools of public speaking, if you'll take these ideas and follow the simple procedures for using these methods, gradually you will learn how to speak in public.

Learning effective public speaking is comparable to learning how to swim. Can a book teach you how to swim? Not if you only read it in your easy chair. But if you do follow its instructions, if you go to a shallow pool of water and do the exercises, chances are you can learn how to swim that way.

How This Book Came to be Written

In the summer of 1980 I organized a two-week course for a group of men and promised to teach them three skills, one of which was public speaking. I had assumed that I easily would find someone who could teach this. After interviewing a number of well-known public speakers, I realized that they were likely to intimidate the students. A polished professional may have little patience to nurture the bumbling student. To my mind, effective public speaking is based on being comfortable with your audience, your material and yourself. Therefore, a teacher who would dramatically announce to the class the seventeen things the student did wrong in his speech may improve the student's speaking ability by five percent... but he has torpedoed the student's self-confidence by fifty percent. When a person is lacking self-confidence, he or she cannot speak authoritatively or comfortably.

As I had little alternative, I undertook a study of public speaking methods and constructed a program of study that made sense. Its guidelines were quite simple:

1. Have every participant speak at least once every session.

2. Don't criticize.

3. Provide opportunities for the participant to see and model good speaking methods.

Since that time, I have taught hundreds of people of all ages and backgrounds, using these basic steps.

Over the years, many ideas to help the student have been added and the program has been fine-tuned. But the basic concepts remain the same.

To enable the student to continue improving on his own, I wrote a manual that was used for many years and is incorporated in this book.

You are getting a proven method. Over the years I have read many books, taken courses, and listened to many cassette programs on the subject of public speaking. I have carefully filtered out the information which is unimportant or which just makes no sense. What has been included are methods that work. They worked for my students, and they'll work for you.

Admittedly, practicing in front of a class of empathetic colleagues is the ideal way to learn public speaking, and you will be given a few suggestions about how to do that. If organizing a group is not possible, however, you can become a very good speaker with the use of two great tools: a cassette player or a video recorder. Using these, you can listen to your speech in the privacy of your own home, review it, correct it, and improve it.

The video allows you even greater opportunity to see the total impact you make in your presentation.

So we're ready. You have your determination to become a public speaker, a book of proven methods, and a cassette player (or video) to enable you to improve.

Congratulations… you're on the right track!

Where Do We Go From Here?

The purpose of this book is to acquaint you with the tools of public speaking and to take you through the steps. You can become a good public speaker by following a relatively simple five-step plan, and then repeating the steps over and over again:

      1. Prepare

      2. Practice

      3. Deliver

      4. Evaluate

      5. Improve

The beauty of this plan is that if you are really determined, you can carry it through yourself. You can challenge yourself to speak on a topic, research and prepare a speech, practice it in an empty room, find or create an opportunity to actually deliver the speech, and then, with the aid of a cassette player or video camera, self-evaluate it.

While working on your own is possible, you'll do much better if you organize a small group of people who will meet each week to practice speaking. Each participant delivers a three- to four-minute speech and then there is a general discussion by the group about how to improve the speeches. If the group wants to include some reading on a topic or discussion of a motivational book, so much the better.

Learning how to become a good and then a great public speaker doesn't require any special or expensive equipment or background. You can improve your vocabulary by reading several pages a day of anything that interests you, looking up each new word, and then using the newly learned words in your casual conversations. (There are books and cassette programs that can enhance this process.) After you are comfortable with the new words, you can use them in a prepared speech.

Remember the Five-Step Plan:
Prepare, Practice, Deliver, Evaluate, Improve

Chapter Two

IT ALL STARTS WITH YOUR ATTITUDE

*P*ublic speaking is perhaps one of the most overrated skills: yet it can be learned by an intelligent person in a relatively short time. While few people would consider driving a car or using a computer without instruction and practice, many people expect to speak in public with no instruction and no guidance. When they don't speak well or are nervous, they conclude . that, "public speaking is not for me" and join the seventy percent of the population who passionately fear public speaking.

The Born Public Speaker

If we need anything to reinforce our conviction that we're not meant to be public speakers, watching one who speaks seemingly effortlessly, enjoys it, and does a great job of public speaking confirms our belief. We label him the "Born Speaker," and we tell ourselves, "He does a good job because he was born with a gift. But I, who was not born with that talent, can't speak in public." If we extend the logic of this thinking, we can further deduce that since we don't have the natural qualities, going to a class or getting training will not make any difference. So why even try? There is a basic mistake in this thinking.

Most of the people who make powerful, polished speeches have paid the price in learning how to do it. Many of today's well-known speakers, who earn thousands of dollars for a single speech, began by speaking for no payment to audiences of ten and twenty people. They may have rehearsed their presentations tens of times, listened carefully to the critique of their friends, practiced again, and delivered hundreds of speeches before reaching the level of proficiency that you admire. Simply stated, these people became professionals because they did the things that most people don't want to do.

It should be noted that, like every rule, there are exceptions. Perhaps five percent of public speakers who reached professional levels do so without paying the painful practice price. But most of us are in the ninety-five percent group, which is comprised of people who have to be taught the skill and who practice it to become proficient! It would be a tremendous mistake to allow the ease with which people with natural ability do things determine which skills you want to acquire.

Yes, You Can

The bottom line is that if you can speak to a person across a desk or on a telephone, you can learn how to speak in public. It will require learning some new ideas and a little risk-taking; but this book can help change speaking in public from a frightening experience to a pleasant, invigorating experience that you will thoroughly enjoy! Follow this easy, step-by-step process, and you, like hundreds of students of all ages, can become a comfortable, competent, effective public speaker.

Why Learn to Speak in Public?

There are a number of reasons why a person may want to learn how to speak effectively in public. In addition to acquiring the confidence to say "yes" when you are asked to speak publicly, there are a number of other benefits that can improve the quality of your life. Not all of these apply to every person, but see how many apply to you.

1. **Effective public speaking will enable you to inspire people.**
   Whether it is a small group with whom you want to share a Torah thought, or a large group you want to involve in a major project, you'll need to motivate people. The best way to achieve your goal is by learning how to "sell" your ideas, and effective public speaking becomes the vehicle.

2. Public speaking will sharpen your thinking abilities.

Just as writing crystallizes thought, proper preparation and delivery of a speech forces you to clarify your thoughts. When you learn to anticipate the audience's questions and strive to develop answers to those questions, your thinking will develop on a solid foundation.

3. Knowing how to speak publicly enables you to reduce frustrations.

Have you ever come home from a meeting "bottled up" with ideas, suggestions, and comments? "I should have told them..." is the refrain of a frustrated person who hasn't learned how to present his opinion publicly.

4. You will build self-confidence.

Self-confidence is important to the well being of a well-rounded person, and there are few ways to build self-confidence as quickly and easily as learning how to speak effectively in public.

5. You will become more active.

You'll change from a passive observer to a person who makes things happen. Just knowing you have the ability to present your ideas clearly, convincingly, and powerfully puts you in a different position. Just knowing that you can speak up if you want to is a reassuring feeling.

6. You will become more interesting.

You'll develop a heightened sensitivity to interesting material once you think of yourself as a "speaker," and you'll discover a new appreciation for everything you read, hear and see. You will start collecting apt thoughts, interesting ideas, concepts, stories and even humorous anecdotes, because you may want to use these in a future presentation. Any article in a magazine or newspaper, a rabbi's sermon, a speech, or even casual conversation with a friend can hold a gem of a thought that you can adopt. Thus, you become a more interested and interesting person. After a while, you will find yourself with a treasure chest of stories, ideas, thoughts, and concepts that will upgrade the quality of your life.

7. You will teach Torah.

You'll have more opportunities to fulfill the *mitzvah* of teaching Torah because every time you're asked to speak in public you can share with your audience a Torah thought or story. You will have the chance not only to teach Torah — which in itself is a great *mitzvah* — but also to reach out to those who are not yet committed to a Torah lifestyle.

8. You will increase your personal pleasure.

Just think of the dozens of personal *simchos* where it will be appropriate and desirable for you to speak. A student told me that the joy he had in speaking at his son's Bar Mitzvah was worth all the effort!

9. You will advance in your career.

Whether you are in education, the rabbinate, private business, government or organizational work, you'll have more opportunities to move ahead when you can represent yourself and your employer confidently in public. Because so many people do not want to speak in public, your value to your company or institution rises when you become known as a speaker.

10. **Public speaking will prepare you for leadership.**

    One of the traits that most leaders have is the ability to inspire people, and public speaking is the easiest, most effective way to inspire many people quickly.

    In fact, you will be able to address the highest aspect of man — his intellect — which is a noble skill. Just think of a banquet of delicious food, elegant service, beautiful flowers, and pleasurable music, all in exquisite surroundings. Most of these elements — food, service, flowers, music, and ambience — address the physical needs of a person. It is speech that addresses the soul.

Excuses, and How to Override Them

How many of these mental excuses have you used to avoid speaking in public?

I am more effective behind the scenes.

While it is possible to become a mover and shaker behind the scenes — motivating other people to do things — for the most part, this reason is a comfortable excuse. My challenge to you is to learn how to speak effectively in public. Then you'll be able to judge in which position you can do better. Until you can speak well, you'll never know where you'll do better.

I don't have a good memory.

You need not memorize a speech. In this book you'll be shown methods that don't require any memorization.

I don't have a large vocabulary.

You don't need to use large, sophisticated words. You just need words that convey your thoughts. In fact it is the small, power-packed action words that move audiences.

I can't think fast on my feet.

Neither do many great public speakers. We don't shoot from the hip, nor do we use what "comes to mind." The professional speech is a carefully thought out presentation.

I can't tell jokes.

You're ahead of the game if you know that you can't tell jokes. It's better than having the audience let you know! The fact is you don't need jokes to speak well. Nevertheless, you will learn some easy ways to make your audience laugh.

I once spoke and I was a complete flop.

You probably fell off a bicycle as you learned how to ride a bike, or got a mouthful of water before you learned how to swim, but these setbacks didn't discourage you. That is the price of learning! But you need not make your mistakes in public while you are learning to speak effectively. You will learn how to lower the risk so that you don't have to be embarrassed.

I don't have anything interesting to say.

There are many places to find interesting and exciting ideas on any given subject. It requires some research, a little reading, and talking to knowledgeable people. All of these efforts are good for you: they will add zest and interest to your life.

I don't have opportunities to speak.

If you have never played the violin, I can't imagine that you have been asked to play the violin. Once you acquire the tools to speak in public, you will find (and create) speaking opportunities.

I am too nervous to stand up in public.

"I'm afraid I'll go blank!" Once you make a commitment to learn how to speak in public, you'll learn how to overcome every problem.

Thousands of people have been taught how to speak effectively and comfortably. You can learn too!

Good public speaking results from good private thinking.

"I'm Better When I'm Spontaneous"

There are only two types of speakers who are effective spontaneously. The first type is The Rare Exception: people who, totally unprepared, can make a speech that is well structured, entertaining, and even informative. They are blessed with a "gift of gab" that needs no warm-up; the right words just come to them at the right times. I would venture to estimate that such people represent less than one percent of public speakers (and they usually don't read instructional books). Moreover, even this very unusual kind of person who can give a good speech spontaneously, could give a great speech with some preparation.

The second type of effective spontaneous speaker is the one who has given hundreds of speeches. His "spontaneous" speech is really just a repeat of a presentation that he worked on in the past.

Imagine that I invited you to my home for a festive meal. You would rightfully expect that the shopping, preparing and cooking would have been done in advance. (In many respects, the amount of preparation is a good indication of the level of respect and admiration the host has for a guest.) If the total preparation was just a flurry of activity prior to the meal, you can expect either a tuna fish sandwich or something previously prepared that has been defrosted and warmed in the microwave.

Those are the two choices in meal preparation, and they are the same two choices in speech presentation. Until you have spoken hundreds of times and have many thoughts and ideas in your "mental freezer," chances are that if you wing it, you will be serving "mental sandwiches." They may suffice in some situations, but they surely don't honor your audience.

In their early years, the real pros wrote every speech down word for word — and many still do it after years of practice. Do this two weeks in advance of your speech date, and you'll have the luxury of reviewing your speech, measuring each word, and considering changes, substitutions or enrichment. Then you will be able to practice it, and move to the next step of writing just the key words or thoughts and using these as the notes for your speech.

How much you respect something is defined by how much you prepare for it.

Chapter Three
YOUR AUDIENCE

Who Is The Audience?

*B*efore we begin to gather material for our speech, before we put pencil to paper, we want to know as much as we can about the audience.

When we know all about the audience, our preparation may be entirely different, or perhaps with just a new slant. Either way, we will be able to plug in directly to the audience — not above them, below them, or to the side.

HELP

I remember a student in our speech course who was excited because he had accepted an invitation to speak at a Shabbos group. He began to prepare an intricate presentation. Since his speech date was several weeks away, I suggested that he go to the group that coming Shabbos and see his audience for himself.

He came back the next week with a whole new approach. He realized that his preparation had been for a young, sophisticated audience, when in fact he would be addressing a group of elderly, rather unlearned people. Had he continued to prepare without knowing his audience, he would have spoken considerably above them.

Here are some questions you would want answered before you begin to prepare your speech:

1. Who will be in the audience — men, women, children? While it is obvious that a speech is prepared differently if it is to be presented to adults or children, there are also subtle differences if the audience is to be all male, all female, or a mixture.

2. What is the average age of the audience? Will they be mainly an older group with a few younger people, or will they be a younger group, possibly with a few older people? Not only will their areas of interest be different, your presentation, stories, and examples should all be more specifically geared to the age-level interests of the listeners.

3. What is the educational background of the average audience member? Are they high school graduates, college graduates, professionals? If the speech is going to be of a religious nature, it is important that you know the religious background of the audience. Does the audience know Hebrew or Yiddish? Will they understand a Jewish expression? How well read are they? What are their areas of interest?

4. What is the political leaning of your audience? This may not be important if your speech has no political overtones, but if you will be touching on any political areas, you should have a good idea of the political convictions of your audience. Will they agree or disagree with you?

5. Where will the audience be coming from and going to? If your audience has just been exposed to a long, tedious exhibit or to five other speakers, your speech will be different than if you're the first speaker. If your audience is rushing off to make a plane or to attend another event, you know that you will not enjoy great attention unless you do something spectacular. You may have more listeners at the beginning of your speech, and therefore you may want to put the most important points up front.

6. Are there any specific areas that should not be discussed? You may find that the audience has just had a lecture on a specific subject or that something happened in town that makes certain subjects unpleasant.

    A speaker told me that he wanted to make a point relevant to the audience by using the example of a local business, not knowing that the business had recently declared bankruptcy. The serious point the speaker wanted to prove with the example turned into a laughing matter. You would be wise to discuss any local issues with a person who knows the score.

7. Are there any specific areas they want discussed? Sometimes a speaker loses a good opportunity to make a point that is

particularly valid for the audience if he is not aware of their specific needs.

Getting Answers to these Important Questions

The obvious answer is to ask the person who is asking you to speak. A good idea is to ask these questions even before you agree to speak. Either way, don't be afraid to ask and ask again, until you get answers that give you an accurate picture of your audience.

The thrust of your questions should be, "I need the answers to these questions so I can best serve your needs." If you aren't satisfied by the answers, or if you feel that some of the answers may have been off target, don't hesitate to call a second or third person.

I have heard chair-people expressing appreciation for the care and effort a speaker takes in asking all these questions. Remember that the best speech presented to the wrong audience doesn't do the job. It is your task to make sure you know the audience.

Are There Captive Audiences?

There is no such thing as a truly "captive audience." We refer to an audience that has no easy or polite way of escaping as a captive audience. As examples, we may think of an audience in a synagogue, classroom, or at a Sheva Brachos. We can reason that since it is impolite for a congregant to leave in the middle of a rabbi's sermon, or since we ate the Sheva Brachos meal, we "owe" it to listen to the speaker. Since the student can't leave the classroom (without incurring penalties!), he will listen to the teacher. In these situations, we tend to believe that the audience is "captive" and must listen.

This is just not true. The audience may physically be sitting in front of us — they may even be looking directly at us — but they can instantly turn off their minds. The fact that our audience is physically restricted in no way lessens our obligation to speak well and maintain their interest.

The obligation to present material in an organized, exciting, and stimulating way is always the speaker's job. It is the speaker's task to engage the audience's attention and keep it from wandering. But this is not as difficult as it sounds.

The Meiri (a rabbinic sage of the thirteenth century) wrote that it's the obligation of the speaker who wants to teach Torah to present the material so that it will be as sweet to the listener as "milk and honey mixed together." If the speaker doesn't present it that well, then it is better not to speak!

The purpose of the above paragraphs is not to intimidate you, but rather to clarify the mission. Most confusion can be traced to the lack of clearly identified objectives. To eliminate confusion in preparing your speech, it would be to your advantage to know from the very beginning that it is your obligation to develop and maintain the audience's interest.

The result of this understanding is a relatively easy-to-use yardstick with which you can evaluate your presentation. "Will this opening Chazal, story, example, joke, argument, testimony, interest my audience or not?" is the measure.

If you adopt this measure as your gold standard and use it constantly, you have taken an enormous leap toward becoming an effective speaker.

The Anticipated Lecture vs. the Imposed Speech

Imagine that you have heard that a wonderful speaker has come to your community and will deliver a talk on a topic you enjoy. You mark the date on your calendar, rearrange your day to get there on time, buy your ticket and settle back for an enlightening lecture. If that speaker comes to the podium, says a few light words and leaves after twenty minutes, you will feel cheated. You had come specifically to hear him speak. You expected at least forty-five minutes of insights and wit.

Now imagine that you are attending a Bar Mitzvah reception and the Bar Mitzvah boy has just delivered the speech his father wrote for him. You expected this; listening to this mandatory address is a price you expected to pay. But what's this? The boy's uncle now approaches the podium and speaks for not five, not ten, but twenty insufferable minutes! Next, his brother has a few clever words to say. Then comes the grandfather, with a sheaf of papers in his hand... In this case, the speeches are imposed on the audience, who may or may not be listening.

In short, take circumstances into account. If you are an invited guest speaker, you can be confident that the audience has come to hear you and you have the obligation to make it worth their while. But if you find yourself addressing an audience whose primary reason for being in that room is not to hear you, save your breath and your reputation by keeping your talk very (and I mean very — two to four minutes) brief.

Chapter Four
SPEECH PREPARATION

Food for the Mind

*T*he preparation and presentation of a speech can be compared in many ways to the preparation and service of a meal. Think of a meal as food for the body, and a speech as food for the mind. Just as the person who prepares food must first consider what his guest will eat and how he can make it desirable, so too the person who prepares a speech must answer these questions: What will my audience listen to? How can I make it pleasurable?

If guests don't eat the food, the body will receive no nutritional value or enjoyment. It makes no difference who prepared the food or how much money or effort it cost. The first rule in food service is "Prepare and serve good food that your guest will eat!" If this is true about food for the body, which we must have in order to function, how much more so does it apply to "food for the mind," which to most people is optional.

Must a speech have "real content"? Yes, if you want the opportunity to nourish the mind; no, if all you want to do is provide some light entertainment. Just as a well-prepared speech with rich material is comparable to a well-balanced, vitamin-packed meal, a light, entertaining speech is comparable to chewing gum. The mouth moves, there is some sweet flavor, but nothing fills the stomach. There are times for chewing gum, but not when the need is for a nourishing meal.

How can you provide nourishment for the mind? By collecting inspirational material. Many people are at their best when they are inspired by something and are able to share that inspiration with the audience. If you are a person who can get excited by an idea, a new concept, or a message, you'll become a more powerful speaker if you learn how to capture that moment of inspiration and share it with the audience.

Have you ever seen someone burst into a room and say, "Boy, do I have great news to tell you!" As a speaker, I don't want to break rudely into an audience's tranquility with that type of announcement... but I do want to capture that energy and enthusiasm to propel my speech.

The real challenge is to find the right inspirational thought when you need it. There are two ways to do this. The hard way is to begin looking for it just a few days before your speech. Although sometimes you may happen to fall upon just the right concept, most often you will spend hours searching for that elusive thought. If this happens when you can least afford the luxury of time, you'll feel the pressure build.

The easy way to find the right inspirational thoughts is to "capture" them at other times — when you read, study, or listen to a speaker — and then write them down for future use.

If you were once excited by a thought, chances are that the same thought will inspire you a second and third time. By keeping a cumulative file of such thoughts, you'll have a treasury of readily available, proven inspirational thoughts.

I once interviewed a rabbi who had a reputation as an exceptional speaker. When I asked him where he got his material, he pointed to a bookcase of *seforim* and English books and asked me to glance at a few of them. Each book had notes written in the margins, and many sentences were highlighted. He told me that whenever he learns a *sefer* or reads a book, in the back of his mind he is thinking, "What can I share with my congregants?" Over the years he has collected hundreds of quotes, stories, and insights that are inspirational.

The easy way to find the right inspirational thoughts is to "capture" them at other times — when you read, study, or listen to a speaker — and then write them down for future use.

When Do You Start To Prepare?

Two people are asked to speak at an event six weeks away. The first person puts it out of his mind until a few days before the event. He then starts to collect all the information that he can and begins to formulate his speech.

Our second friend starts to collect information immediately on the subject of the speech and allows this material to "percolate" in his mind for a few weeks. There are considerable advantages gained using the second method:

1. The material becomes "yours." I once sat at a wedding and told the guests at my table a funny story, to which they all responded with loud laughter. Within a minute after I finished the story, the person sitting next to me was asked to say a few words. Although he knew in advance that he would be called upon to speak and was prepared, he chose to start his speech with the funny story he had just heard — and it was a disaster. The speaker's funny story fell flat because he had no time to make it "his." He was just repeating someone else's story, and it came across as dry and uninteresting. That's an extreme example, but nevertheless a good one, because it teaches us a powerful lesson: to be most effective, you have to feel comfortable with the material. This includes any facts, jokes, stories, thoughts, or anything else you say. It has to fit your style, and you have to present it at your speed and with your special "spin."

To obtain the full flavor of a premium coffee bean, you have to allow time for the boiling water to slowly unlock the flavor and essence, a process we call percolating; so too, to fully appreciate and develop the potential of each piece of material, the mind needs time to turn it over, play with it and compose it. You can't force the process, and it can't be done quickly.

2. By starting to work immediately on the speech, you challenge your mind to tune in to anything even remotely usable. A casual conversation or an unrelated newspaper article might suddenly produce a thought you can use. Once it has been given clear instructions, the mind is surprising in its almost magnetic ability to attract information you need.

When Pride Prevents Preparation

Here is a true story related to me by a successful lawyer who had just returned from a charity Melavah Malkah. He and his wife had hired a baby sitter, traveled for half an hour, and braved the cold January weather to attend this affair. The Melavah Malkah was an enjoyable event. The couple met many friends, had good food, enjoyable entertainment... all the ingredients of a pleasant evening.

The guest speaker was a well-known person who had a wide range of public-speaking experiences. He spoke for forty-five minutes to an audience that was respectful and listened intently. He told a few interesting stories, a good *vort*, a funny joke, yet he left many guests disappointed.

I quote my friend: "The speech was good, but if he had prepared, it could have been great! I felt as if he had casually, almost incidentally, pulled together whatever came to his mind. Because he has such a large repertoire of material, it was passable, but it lacked a theme, it had no beginning nor ending; it didn't have a unified idea or a central message."

Ironically, this public speaker is an acquaintance of mine, and I know that he prides himself on not having to prepare anymore!

If a hungry person came unexpectedly to your home and you opened the refrigerator to take out whatever is at hand, your guest would eventually be satiated. But you can't compare an assortment of leftovers to a planned, coordinated meal.

Feeding an unexpected visitor whatever you have would be acceptable hospitality. But if you knew in advance that he is coming, especially if he is an important guest, and then you feed him whatever is available, no doubt he will feel insulted.

I'm sure there were many on that Saturday night for whom that guest speaker's speech was adequate. With just a few minutes of forethought and perhaps a half-hour of preparation, however, he could have made it so much better, something that would reach and uplift everyone. The man who told me this story wanted to be inspired; but the speaker's lack of preparation left him disappointed.

Define Your Goals

To prepare a good speech, you should first clearly define the answers, in your own mind, to the following four questions:

1. What is the purpose of the speech?

The preparation of a speech involves ideas, their organization, and their realization into words. The first step is to decide upon the basic purpose of the speech and the type of response desired from the audience, since the choice and treatment of the subject depend on these factors.

Is the purpose of the speech to inform, entertain, persuade, convince, actuate, impress or teach? Sometimes it may be a combination of two or more of the above. Define each and every purpose of your speech. Write out as clearly as you can the specific objective or multiple objectives. Example: "My objective is to share an interesting story (entertain); to strengthen the audience's belief in a person's ability (convince, impress); and to motivate the audience to take a specific action, by voting for a particular candidate (actuate)."

Let's briefly discuss each of the above purposes.

To Inform

Much public speaking is done to convey information, to satisfy curiosity, or to make things clear. We all have a strong desire for information; to know what is happening in the neighborhood, the country, the world; to understand the nature of things, to learn about the activities and achievements of other people. The typical informative speech describes, explains, defines or demonstrates something. Topics may include news about a new company policy, developments in the field of education, what to look for when buying used cars, how to pack a suitcase, or unusual places to vacation.

To Entertain

Some speeches are designed to amuse listeners by putting them in a pleasant frame of mind, and are suitable on such occasions as dinners, meetings and informal affairs. Personal experiences, human foibles, and pretensions in marriage, politics or other institutions are just a few of a wide variety of topics. Illustrated talks on arts and crafts are colorful examples of speeches to entertain, as are exhibits of objects collected as a hobby.

The traditional format of the entertaining speech is the story or narrative. Adventure stories and success stories have never lost their appeal. Accounts of mishaps, lucky breaks and discoveries offer the pleasure of escape from the pressures of daily living.

To Persuade

Many speeches are made to influence the beliefs, feelings, or conduct of others by getting them to change or intensify their inclinations and points of view. Persuasion, in turn, can have the following aims:

▸ To Convince

The aim of a speech to convince is to alter or strengthen the opinions of the listeners. The speaker appeals to the minds of the audience and induces belief in an idea by offering proof. Proof consists of facts, judgments of experts, logical arguments and a judicious manner of presentation. The following are representative topics for a speech to convince: The town's need for a new park, the high price of government, or the wonderful benefits of volunteering.

▸ To Actuate

A speech to actuate influences listeners to perform a specific deed. The act may have political, social, economic, or personal value.

A speaker has no authority to command an audience, and a mere request, even by an influential person, would probably be ignored. Listeners perform an action only when they believe it is to their own satisfaction or advantage to do so! The speaker must give convincing reasons for the action and proof of the result in order to stimulate the listener's desire to perform it. The following are examples of specific actions targeted in speeches of this nature: vote for a candidate; contribute to a charity; buy an item; perform daily exercises; give up smoking; write to the city authorities to place a traffic light at a dangerous crossing; sign a petition against constructing a factory in a residential area.

To Impress

A speech to impress stimulates the feelings and emotions of the listeners, reinforces their appreciation of moral, aesthetic, or social values, or inspires them with great ideas and experiences.

Listeners can be inspired to greater efforts of their own and to a deeper appreciation of life by examples of great men and women who are devoted to the ideals of service to mankind or who have achieved great things in life. A eulogy is a good example of this kind of speech.

To Teach (or to Share)

The invitation to speak, whether it is for three minutes or an hour, is an opportunity to share your time and thoughts with the audience. It is a wonderful chance to impart an inspiring thought, an uplifting idea or a moving story in a positive frame of reference.

In a society in which the negative values are usually prominently displayed and in which the media usually focuses on the deviant few, there are many opportunities, as well as a great need, for a speaker to offer a few refreshing, wholesome and inspirational comments.

2. Where will I be speaking?

Will the speech take place in the dining room of the company cafeteria, local restaurant, or the board of directors' room? Is it a formal occasion where you will follow other speakers and where you will be introduced, or will it be totally informal?

All of these factors have an effect on the tonal quality of the speech, and you should know about them before you begin to prepare.

3. How much time is allocated?

This is one factor that can make a great difference in your preparation.

> **It's better to speak very well for a short time than poorly for a long time!**

Deliver one central thought well, perhaps just one story, and it will be more effective, better appreciated, and longer remembered than a drawn-out, poorly organized speech. Look to condense, to tighten your draft so that it flows and finishes exactly on time, or even before. Example: The time allocated is five minutes. This will allow you half a minute for an opening, four minutes for the message, and half a minute for a closing.

The amount of time allotted for a speech will, to a large extent, determine what you can possibly do. In general, a two-minute speech allotment will allow for warm greetings; five minutes for the explanation of an idea; ten to fifteen minutes for the presentation of a whole concept, allowing for an adequate introduction, body, and summary.

Notwithstanding what other speakers do, and regardless of the fact that "five minutes" traditionally runs fifteen or twenty minutes, stay exactly within your allotted time! Few things so frustrate those who are responsible for the smooth flowing of an affair (chairman, president, caterer) as a string of speakers who each uses five, ten, or fifteen minutes more than their allotted time. Many times, dinners are scheduled to the minute, with meal service and entertainment carefully planned. The speaker who abuses his allotted time often causes untold problems for others involved in the affair.

When you are asked to speak, assure the chairman that you will keep your time schedule to the minute. Then ask him exactly how long he wants you to speak. (Let him tell you the real time allotment after you've convinced him you will keep to it.) Practice your speech so that it fits exactly into the promised time, or is perhaps even a little shorter. Do not try to cram too much material into too short a time. If you have been given only two minutes, give a greeting. It is better to give a carefully prepared, fully practiced, well-presented, two-minute greeting than to try to put three or four "just-one-more" stories into an already crowded speech.

Practice your speech so that it fits exactly into the promised time, or is perhaps even a little shorter.

4. What is the occasion?

Given different occasions, not only should your message differ, but so should the opening, the closing, and the tonal quality. It's important to clearly identify the mood your audience will probably be in. Try to visualize what your audience's physical and emotional situation will be at the moment when you get up to speak. Did they just eat a heavy dinner, enjoy two martinis and listen to five speeches? Your task of holding their attention in that case will be considerably different than if you were to speak to the same audience as the first speaker at ten o'clock in the morning.

The Mechanics of a Speech: Three Easy Steps

There are three easy steps to preparing a speech and delivering it well.

1. Think through carefully what to say.
2. Prepare an outline.
3. Practice it until it comes naturally.

The following guidelines will help you through each step.

1. Think it Through

Regardless if it is a two-minute greeting, a twenty-minute speech, or a two-hour presentation, all properly prepared speeches need three components to flow smoothly:

A. An opening

B. A message

C. A closing

A. The Opening

The opening of a speech must do two things: it must establish a mood, a rapport between audience and speaker, and it must earn the speaker the right to the audience's attention. The way you walk up to the lectern, the way you stand, your tone, all say to the audience, "This person is knowledgeable and confident; his message must be important."

The opening should set the mood. It should build a bridge of confidence between you and your audience. This is especially true when you are addressing an audience on a subject that could make them feel uncomfortable, such as an appeal, a challenge to their way of thinking or their lifestyle or if you are advocating something that may be unpopular. A good opening says, "Don't worry, I'm on your side. I understand you, I identify with you, I like you, I'm part of you!"

The opening holds out the promise (which you intend to deliver!) of added information; interesting stories; provocative, engaging thoughts; useful information and an enjoyable time.

You don't have to (and should not) announce any of these intentions to your audience in your opening, but properly executed the message will come through. (See the chapter about

"Six Messages We Want to Send to Our Audiences – Without Saying So.")

Within the first minute or two of a speech, your audience will decide, consciously or unconsciously, "This speaker is good! Interesting! I have much to learn from this speech!" Or they may decide, "This speech is not for me — I can go to sleep." So the first minute or two of the opening is extremely important. Here are several ideas for openings:

- ▸ Arouse curiosity.
- ▸ Tell a story.
- ▸ Give a specific illustration.
- ▸ Use an exhibit.
- ▸ Ask a question.
- ▸ Begin with a fascinating quote.
- ▸ State a shocking fact.

Never apologize. An apology is a negative format and calls your audience's attention to your lack of something: your lack of preparation, the fact that you cannot control your time, the fact that you did not consider your audience important enough to prepare well. Whatever the lack, the connotation is negative.

If you are really unprepared and cannot speak, don't!

Never say you are here to speak: it is obvious. Don't make a foolish statement or false introduction that may mislead your audience.

Try to find a pleasing, positive point with which to start. Find a specific reason why you're happy to be here; a special reason why you have the desire, the right, or the privilege to speak at this occasion. Reach out to the audience, share an interesting observation with them.

The opening of a two-minute speech may be only a fifteen-second sentence thanking your host for allowing you to speak, but it can also say, "I'm really glad to be here, and to be able to join in this *simchah* with all of you." The length of the opening is not crucial, the tone is! Be positive, friendly and enthusiastic.

Let the way you walk up to the podium say, "This speech is a pleasure I look forward to," not, "This speech is a burden I want to get rid of."

Let your tone say, "Give me just a few minutes of your time, listen to me with an open mind and I will make your time and effort worthwhile."

B. The Message

If your opening "sets the stage," your message is the performance, the reason you took the trouble to set the stage in the first place. The purpose of the opening is to position and prepare your audience, mentally and emotionally, for the message. Now they are ready — give it to them! Ideally there should be a natural tie-in between the opening and the message. They should follow and flow one into the other.

If the opening aroused curiosity, asked a question, or presented a shocking fact, your message must explain, expand, back up and deliver the idea. The delivery will be based on the purpose of your speech:

To Inform: Now that your opening warmed them up, build your case! Start at a logical beginning and build up your information block by block. Stop at some point to allow your audience to mentally "catch their breath." If it's a long presentation, allow for a review at midpoint. Use charts to illustrate any complex material.

To Persuade: Now that your opening made the audience your friends, present your facts and persuade. Explain the problem, outline your argument, and then bring proof, perhaps by quoting authentic testimonial letters, or by citing names.

To Convince: After your opening has said to the audience, "I'm on your side, and I'm here for your benefit," now ride the momentum and convince them. Put yourself in your listener's position, in his or her frame of reference. Why should s/he agree? Just because you say so? What would it take to convince you in a similar situation? Try out your proofs on your spouse and on your friends. Can you convince them of your point with the proof and logic you presented?

To Teach: After your opening has developed an understanding, a closeness between you and your audience, they are ready for the development of an idea. Make sure your starting point does not make an inaccurate presumption about your audience's level, whether higher or lower.

Explain your questions well. Ask the question with such clarity, with such impact, that the audience will desperately want to know the answer. Then tell the entire story correctly and clearly.

Once you develop this method of thinking, you will be amazed at how much you can present in a few minutes. It's better to pack a lot into a few minutes than to stretch out a weak presentation over a long time.

C. The Closing

The closing is the signature of the expert. Its purpose is to round out the speech, to tie it all up neatly, to charge the audience with specific action or direction and to set the audience gently back in its seat.

Don't talk about stopping: just prepare to stop, no differently than when you bring a car to a gradual, slow, smooth stop after a drive.

Here are several suggestions for how to conclude your speech:

- ▸ Summarize your points.
- ▸ Appeal for action.
- ▸ Pay the audience a sincere compliment.
- ▸ Capture in one line the kernel of your speech.
- ▸ Use a famous quote.

The closing may well be the part your audience will best remember, so plan it carefully.

2. Prepare An Outline

An outline is the visual record of a systematically organized thought structure. When the speaker has selected, limited, and divided his subject, determined its specific purpose, and gathered and arranged supporting materials, he has already done much of the mental work of outlining. The main ideas of the subject become the main headings of the outline, and the subordinate ideas become the subheadings. The remaining supporting materials are recorded in their proper places. Making an outline puts the results of the speaker's analysis and synthesis on paper.

3. Practice, Practice!

Ideally, you should never read a speech, or even memorize it word for word. Few things so distract an audience as a speaker who reads a speech, and nothing so strains or stilts a speech as when it is recited from memory.

The best method of delivery is to familiarize yourself with, but not to memorize, your speech. You will have written down the key thoughts, and you will have practiced expressing these key thoughts until they come out naturally.

Let's say your opening has two thoughts you wish to express. You outline these, putting them in proper sequence and finding the right key words for them. Develop key phrases, sentences, and words, putting them into the outline.

You may practice the thoughts, the key words, and the delivery twenty times, but the sentences will still come out with a freshness and vibrancy if you learn to use the key phrases rather than memorizing the exact words. If you memorize and practice them word by word, your speech will sound stilted.

There are many ways to practice. Try them all until you find the ones best suited for you. Practice by delivering the speech as a whole, all three sections together.

Take a walk and practice your speech. The great outdoors will allow you to speak loudly and to project your voice. (Don't try this on city streets!)

Practice the message portion in general conversation with a few friends. For example: If the message of your speech is a new idea, you could casually relate this idea to your spouse and several good friends. They are the perfect audience on whom to practice your messages. (Obviously, don't tell them that you're practicing on them!) As you speak to them, listen to how your message sounds and gauge your listeners' reactions to it. Keep refining it until you get your idea across and receive the response you intended.

If you can, get permission to use a large room (perhaps a dining room or a school gym) and practice there. The room, the platform, the mike, will do a lot to bolster your ego and raise your comfort level.

If at all possible, try to practice in the very room in which you will speak. Your familiarity with the room will go a long way toward easing stage fright.

Spend a lot of time practicing the opening... getting up... walking to the lectern... waiting... reciting your first sentence... until you have done it so many times that it becomes second nature.

Remember, every speech, regardless of how insignificant the occasion, if used as practice, becomes another stepping stone to becoming a great speaker.

Practice well and you'll speak well.

A Proven Method for Honing Your Speech

Nothing is more frustrating to a speaker than to be told afterwards by a friend, "That was a great speech. But you should have..."

The problem is, he's right! His suggestion is on the mark and you wonder why you didn't think of it yourself.

There is an easy way to avoid this, though you must be ready to invest a little time and to put away your ego for a while. After you have practiced your speech, record it on tape and give a copy to each of three of your friends. Ask them to critique the speech by listening to it and jotting down ideas, questions and criticisms. After you have these three written lists of suggestions, you can incorporate the best ideas into your speech and rectify any problems that have been pointed out. Now record the speech again, and give it to three other friends! After your speech goes through this refining process three times, you can be pretty sure your speech will meet everyone's expectations. (If you still have any friends left, save them for your next speech.)

How To Organize A Speech

Here are some tips on how to organize your speech easily.

1. Write the last sentence first.

Imagine that you want to take a trip. Before you answer the question "How do I get there?" you must first decide on a destination. You select a place, city, country to visit, and then you consider whether to drive, fly, go by train, bus, boat, or a combination of several modes of travel.

Likewise, in the organization of your speech, you want to know your closing first. What do you want the audience to hear as its last and lasting message? Once you write this sentence, it becomes your destination and your objective. Now you have to find which is the best mode of travel.

Now let us apply this principle. Ask yourself, "To this audience, in this room, at this time, what message do I want to deliver?" That is your destination. After you know where you want to go, consider how to get there. "Do I use a funny story, a joke, an inspirational thought, a *ma'amar Chazal*, a news item, a quote, a life experience, or some combination of these? How will I best reach my objective?"

2. Write the main theme.

You will not always be able to catch the thrust of your speech in just the last sentence. Your theme may require two or three sentences to describe, or it may not be appropriate as a closing.

When your main idea does require several sentences, write these sentences down and consider them the centerpiece of your presentation. A centerpiece is usually the largest of all the displays, but even more importantly, it sets the tone of the display, and all the other pieces of the display are coordinated to it.

Your central theme should do the same thing. All the other elements of the speech — the opening, the closing, the emotional parts, the funny parts — are all measured by the central theme. Will the funny story strengthen the theme if it comes before or after it? Should the central theme be introduced in the first few minutes so that the remainder of the speech can include proof and testimony, or should the central theme appear toward the end, so that you can use the first half of the speech to prepare the audience by sharpening the focus?

3. Organize with a format.

One of the difficulties that a speech must overcome is the inability of the audience to actually see anything. A speech is made of words, and words are invisible. They disappear in the split-seconds that it takes the sound waves to dissipate. You can't go back to hear it again, as you can reread something written on a page. You can't compare something the speaker said two minutes ago to what he said fifteen minutes ago unless you remember both thoughts clearly, something many people find difficult.

Therefore, one of the most efficient ways to help the audience is to provide a set of familiar "hooks" by which they can follow your speech. A few format suggestions:

▸ Time is familiar to all of us. Whether we refer to hours of a day, days of a week, weeks of a month, months of a year, or years of a century, your audience is familiar with it. If the subject of your speech lends itself to it, organize your speech sequentially. You are in a sense saying, "If you follow along a time line with me, you will find it easy to remember."

▸ The next way to provide "hooks" for your audience is to organize your speech so that it follows a logical sequence of space. For example, if you have traveled across the United States and want to speak about several interesting places you saw, do it in accordance with an easy-to-follow route. If your trip started in New York, you would want to go from east to west, or "travel" up or down the eastern seaboard. Your audience can more easily follow such a route. You will find it so much easier to organize and outline a speech if you follow such a plan, instead of jumping from location to location.

▸ Cause and effect is the natural way we see things work. Therefore, if you use "cause," the reason something happened, the story behind the story, and then move on to the effect, you can expect your audience to follow along. You will have accomplished two objectives: your organization of the speech will be relatively easy, and your audience will follow more easily.

▸ Another method is to go step by step. You may find it to your advantage to write your speech as a list, like steps up a staircase.

For example, let's say you are speaking about the steps needed to prepare for travel abroad. To go to a foreign country, you need to have the following considerations:

> Decide on the country.
>
> List all options of travel.
>
> Consider dates, time of year, length of stay.
>
> Consider how you will finance the trip.
>
> Decide what to do there.
>
> Consider the accessory details: language, pictures, etc.

Now, to make the speech, you flesh out each point. You tell the audience all the various ways to gather information on different countries, how to make the decision, etc. The speech should flow in a logical, step-by-step way.

Can you imagine the audience's reaction if the speaker would first discuss what to do in the vacation spot and then jump to a list of travel options, followed by the topic of taking pictures? The audience would be confused without a convenient "hook" to retrieve and remember the information.

> ‣ Make an outline. Since our early school days we can remember the outline: the listing of major topics and the smaller, less important ones under their respective headings.

This is a wonderful and simple way to organize a speech. List in outline form the few major points you wish to make. Under each major point, list a clarification, support, testimony, joke, proverb, *vort*, or story — any item that can clarify and/or make it easier to remember.

After you're done with your outline, all you need to do is examine each piece to see if it is important to your objective, add an interesting beginning and a memorable ending.

> ‣ Use a list. If you say to your audience, "There are six points I want to make," they have a map of where you're going. (Be careful that you have notes that actually list all six points; once you announce a number, you'll be embarrassed if you then list fewer points.)

Writing Vs. Speaking

There is a difference between writing and speaking. Therefore, writing and then just reading a speech can be disastrous. A word can look great on paper and be difficult to pronounce, a phrase can be effective in a written letter but fall flat when spoken, a paragraph can be interesting or even exciting when written, yet hard to understand when read aloud.

Writing and speaking have several basic differences: The written word has a graphic expression to back it. The margins give it a frame of reference, the lines of type can be short or long, the white space can be used to divide the material and give pause between thoughts. Different sizes of type are used to convey a range of varied emotional expressions such as surprise, shock, sensitivity, boldness or timidity. Even on a single typed page, we use commas to separate ideas, underlining to emphasize, bold or capital letters to attract attention.

Moreover, on the printed page you can compare two sentences typed next to each other. You can refer to something on a page that you just read, or turn a page ahead. In a book, you can use illustrations and color to make the presentation more interesting.

While you can't do many of the above in speaking, you can do many other things. You can raise or lower your voice, change pitch, change the rate of speech, charge your words with emotion, stop, pause, laugh, cry, use facial expressions, walk around, use hand gestures. I do not mean to infer that either communication method is limited or that one is more versatile. The point I want to make is that writing and speaking are different. Therefore, you can't hope to write a speech and be effective just by reading it out loud.

Some Advice for the Beginner

In preparing a speech, one needs to write his or her thoughts, to organize them on paper. You will use many sheets of paper to develop and outline your presentation. But when you begin to convert your thoughts into a speech, you should change from the written medium to the spoken. You should begin by writing your speech word by word, but then read it out loud to hear how it sounds. When you find a sentence that doesn't sound good, change it. When you find a sentence that is confusing because it is too long or has too many thoughts, shorten it. You may find a thought difficult to understand because you didn't introduce it properly, and then you'll have to add a sentence.

As you work from your written sheet, you begin to put in timing signals. You may use a slash (/) to indicate a major pause, underline to indicate that you want to say it fast, or and other symbols of your own.

Once you are thoroughly familiar with your speech, transfer the key phrases only to a single sheet of paper to use as your notes. Practice using just these notes. You may want to bring the fully written speech to the podium as a back-up, in case you need to jog your memory. Chances are, you'll never use it!

Time and the Jewish Problem

$\mathbf{A}$lthough it's not usually your option as a speaker, you should always try to start on time. Starting on time says you're a professional. It says that you value your time and respect the audience's time.

To understand this point, just imagine a meeting that is called for eight o'clock. You and three other people are there at eight o'clock. The president, who himself comes in fifteen minutes late, decides, "Since there are only a few of us here, we'll just wait a few more minutes."

What message did you hear? Many people would answer, "The message I heard was, 'People who came at eight o'clock are fools. The real people, the smart people, know not to come early and just sit around. They come at eight-forty, and that's when the action begins.'" You don't have to hear that message too many times to learn to come late yourself.

I don't mean to imply that as a speaker you are responsible for the timing of the program. That responsibility belongs to the chairman. But be aware of the time factor. If you're asked to speak for forty-five minutes and you begin thirty minutes late, more often than not the audience will perceive and remember you as a speaker who spoke for an hour or an hour and a quarter.

In order to be respectful of the time, perhaps you would want to give thought to the possibility of structuring and building your speech in compartments. Let's assume:

A represents your opening remarks

B is the body, the message of your speech

C is a good story that proves the main point

D is another story

E is a joke

F is the summary and closing

When you have the full forty-five minutes, this structure makes good sense. You open with **A**, your thrust is **B**, you support your position with **C**, **D**, and **E**, and close with **F**. But when you judge that you will have the audience's attention for only ten or fifteen minutes, it would be foolhardy to ram a twenty-five-minute presentation down their throats just because you have a twenty-five-minute speech!

Imagine that you prepared a five-course meal that you wanted to enjoy in a leisurely fashion with a friend. You had hoped to slowly savor the special dishes you prepared. You had planned a table wine to be enjoyed between the entree and main dish.

But for some reason beyond your control, your friend arrives late and is in no mood for a leisurely meal. He is hungry and has only half an hour to eat. Do you, as a host, insist that he eat all the food you prepared? I surely hope not! You would be smart to serve the main dish and possibly give him smaller portions. To insist that he eat all the food you prepared, just because you prepared it, is unreasonable and discourteous. You may be able to insist that your friend eat all the

food, but that would amount to force-feeding him and will give him a stomachache.

If you "build" your speech in compartments, you can decide later whether to serve the whole meal or a short version. You could choose to "serve" **A**, **B**, **C**, **D**, **E**, and **F** when you have thirty minutes. **A**, **B**, **D**, and **F** when you have twenty-five minutes, and **A**, **B**, and **F** if you only have fifteen minutes. Obviously, your speech will not flow as smoothly when you use three or four parts as it would if you used all of them. But some practice can help make it a professional presentation either way.

Using an Audience Take-Home Sheet

Imagine the perfect speech. You researched the material, got to know and like your audience, worked hard on the structure, and practiced your presentation. You looked good, felt good and performed beautifully! Your audience gave you a standing ovation: You did it! Now, let's follow a member of the audience home. Mr. Gold goes home and says to his spouse, "I heard a great speaker!"

She responds, "What did he say?

And to our delight he replies, "He made three important points," and then in several succinct sentences, Mr. Gold captures the major thrust of each point.

You have just witnessed the effective execution of both parts of a speech: The giving of a speech (the speaker's job); and the reception of the speech (the listener's response.)

Just as a clear fax is the result of a clearly written letter sent by a perfectly functioning machine to another perfectly functioning machine, so too, a good speech depends on a good message transmitted by an inspired speaker to a fully functioning audience.

The speaker can help the audience understand and remember the major points of his presentation by preparing in advance an Audience Take-Home Sheet.

This device is a sheet of paper on which you write down for yourself the two or three major points that you will make in your presentation, the few sentences that you would want Mr. Gold to tell his wife. If you had the opportunity to put the words in his mouth, what would they be? The opening comment, the story, the joke, the parable may all be enjoyable to listen to, but their purpose is to carry the message. They are not the message itself. If the audience remembers the story and forgets the message, will you as a speaker feel fulfilled? Hopefully, your message is the important payload, like a payload in a rocket; everything else is the delivery system.

When you have clearly written the two or three points that capture the essence of your speech, the ideas that you want your audience to take home with them, you will have taken a giant step toward enabling your audience to absorb the material. The more clearly you have your speech thought through, to the extent of having written out the main point word for word, the better chance you have of reaching your audience and enabling them to repeat the ideas to someone else.

There are some situations, such as a lecture or workshop, where you may want to actually distribute an Audience Take-Home Sheet at the end of your speech. But even when you speak at a banquet or graduation, which do not allow for an Audience Take-Home Sheet, It's good to create one anyway. By preparing it and focusing on the question, "Exactly what do I want my audience to take home?" your speech will then be better structured and more forcefully presented. When you come to one of your points you may want to say, "Here is a major point," or you may say, "If you're taking notes, write this down." Once you have the essence of your speech boiled down to a few key sentences, once you have condensed it to a few vitals, your presentation will be dynamic, clear, to the point.

WORKSHEETS — THE SPEECH ORGANIZER

WORKSHEET A

Developing Your Speech

Use this guide to help you think through each step of your speech. The more clearly you define each objective, the easier it will be for you to develop your speech.

1. Objective

    A. Purpose (to inform, entertain, convince, actuate, other) _____

    B. Who is my audience? _____

    C. Where will I be speaking? _____

    D. How much time is allocated? _____

2. In one sentence, describe concisely and clearly, what you want to say. _____

3. Structure (After completion, carry these over in greater detail to Worksheet B.)

    A. Opening _____

    B. Message _____

    C. Closing _____

4. Time spent in planning speech _____

    Time spent in practicing delivery_____

WORKSHEET B
Key Words

Title of Speech: _____

Key words, phrases and quotes to be used:

    A. Opening _____

    _____

    B. Message _____

    _____

    C. Closing _____

    _____

WORKSHEET C
Audience Take-Home Sheet

Write 1-3 sentences that capture the essence of this presentation.

_____

_____

_____

_____

_____

Chapter Five

SPEECH COMPONENTS AND TECHNIQUES

Telling a Story

*S*tories pack a tremendous amount of human interest. In fact, when the speaker knows his craft, the words "Let me tell you a story" can be an invitation to an exciting experience.

Stories can introduce us to distant countries and customs. They can take us up close to famous and interesting people. They can be dramatic or humorous, and they can be a combination of all of the above.

Ever since we were children, stories have held almost a magical interest for us. A public speaker can easily use this fascination to his advantage. But there is so much more that you can do with a good story.

Many people have developed a resistance to a speech or lecture. The source of this resistance is irrelevant, whether it is learned in school or is the result of having been subjected to a number of badly organized speeches. The net result is that many people in the audience turn off as soon as a lecture or speech begins. But when you begin to tell a story you stand a good chance of breaking out of the lecture mode. Audience resistance is suspended for a short while and if you use this "window of opportunity" to tell a really good story, you may be able to get your point across even to people who usually would not listen.

A story has appeal for all ages and all nationalities. It is easy to listen to and will put the audience in a comfortable, receptive frame of mind.

Here are some ideas to help you perfect your storytelling:

1. Telling a story interestingly is a skill, and you can learn this skill by listening to others do it. Every time you hear a speaker tell a story, listen intently and ask yourself, "What did he do well? How effective was his presentation? What can I learn from him?"

2. Recognize stories in the books that you read and examine how the author presented them. Was the reader given adequate background information? Was the scene described with enough detail? Were unimportant details kept out of the story?

3. Try telling stories in your conversations. If you hear a good story, tell it to the next five people with whom you speak. Get the feel and the fun of telling a story.

4. Learn how to use timing. Timing is crucial in a story. The punch line has to be delivered just right, or you lose the effect. Practice timing until you have it right.

5. Use simple, short stories and don't rush through them. Long stories are often complicated and hard to remember. Short stories that clearly make a point, that have punch and zest, are the ones you want to use.

6. Make sure your story is relevant to the point you want to make. Just because you have a good story is no reason to include it in your speech if the audience will not see its connection to the main idea. A story should reinforce your point or shed new light on it. It can give the audience a new or different way to see your point — but it must revolve around or expand on that point.

7. If your story contains names of people, be doubly careful that there is no overt or covert negative implication. Obviously, you don't want to say something derogatory about anyone, but be careful of implications. Sometimes the use of a phrase, the position of a fact, or a gesture can throw a new meaning on your words. Don't use words for their shock value; you may be embarrassed by the audience's reaction.

Humor

The good news is you don't need to begin a speech with a joke. The bad news is that few speakers believe that! But it is true. On the list of the greatest mistakes speakers can make, misusing humor has to be near the top, and the reason for it is simple. Listening to a polished speaker tell an appropriate joke at just the right moment and getting a hearty laugh is so enjoyable that we all want to do it! Hearing a professional use a humorous story effectively to prove a difficult point is so powerful that we all want to imitate it.

Without recognizing the skill that it takes to get even a casual joke to go over well, many of us use stale, canned humor that has no relevance to the occasion, deliver it badly, and watch it bomb.

Although there are techniques anyone can use to brighten up a speech with some light remarks, let us leave the joke-telling to those who can do it well. If you can't get a few good friends to laugh at your jokes at the breakfast table, don't imagine that the same joke will get three hundred strangers to laugh during a formal speech! So set aside the misconception that you must open a speech with a joke. You don't need jokes or even a funny story to capture or hold the attention of your audience. Remember: Until you develop the skill and timing to do it right, no humor is always better than bad humor.

As I suggested above, however, there are ways you can use light humor, with a bit of practice on your inflections and timing:

1. Describe a cartoon. If you can do this quickly, you may be able to get a few smiles.

2. Read a funny quip. You may get a light moment by reading just a few lines from an article such as the following, which was taken from *The Wall Street Journal*:

   The Art of Lying: Here's how to write recommendations for lousy job candidates.

   For a candidate with interpersonal problems, say: 'I am pleased to say this person is a former colleague of mine.'

   For the lazy worker: 'In my opinion, you will be very fortunate to get this person to work for you.'

   For the criminal: 'He's a man of many convictions' and 'I'm sorry we let her get away.'

   For the untrustworthy candidate: 'Her true ability is deceiving.' And for the inept worker: 'I most enthusiastically recommend this person with no qualifications whatsoever.'

3. Try a few "one-liners." If they are quick (ten to fifteen seconds), even if they fall flat, you can continue as if nothing happened.

Never, never, never tell a joke at someone else's – anyone else's — expense. A joke about a person, institution, organization, or even a community can and will be remembered (and regretted) long after every other thing you said is forgotten.

Don't be sarcastic or cutting. These are not attitudes that endear you to your audience. Be optimistic and positive.

Did You Hear the One About...?

WORD TO THE WISE

Telling a lengthy joke requires great skill. When you choose to tell a long joke or anecdote, you invest a good deal of your speech time in a technique that may fall flat. A quick line carries less risk. In *The Light Touch* (published by Simon and Schuster, 1990), Malcolm Kushner lists seven types of brief humor anyone can use:

1. Cartoons   2. Lists   3. Letters   4. Quotes

5. Analogies   6. Definitions   7. Observations

You may find some of his advice useful in adding sparkle to your speech.

Allow your audience time to laugh or applaud. If you say something that evokes laughter, make sure you don't continue your speech before the audience has had enough time to laugh. If you continue too soon, two things will happen: The first few words of your next sentence will not be heard, and you will signal the audience that you do not expect or even want them to laugh. Moreover, your inability to adjust to the needs of the audience will make your presentation appear stiff and formal.

So relax. When the audience responds with applause, stop, enjoy it, thank them and continue. When the audience responds by laughing, stop, smile as if to say, "I too enjoy the joke" and continue.

The message you're now sending is, "I'm relaxed and am enjoying giving this speech. I want you to relax and enjoy listening to it."

Statistics

Statistics, when they are easy to understand, can drive a message home very powerfully. When we talk about a two-percent change in a gross national product of several billions of dollars to an audience that is concerned about a $298-a-month car payment and a fifteen-dollar late charge, we've not only lost our audience, but in a sense insulted them also.

When a speaker speaks to me in a language that I don't understand, uses concepts that I don't understand or uses words that I don't understand, the message is either: "This speech is not for you," or worse yet, "You're too stupid to understand my message!" While I may fully realize that the speaker does not mean to insult me, my gut reaction is to feel insulted.

Thus, the general rule is to make sure that everything you say is clear; the specific rule is that all statistics should be easily understood by your audience. Obviously, if you're speaking to a group of CPA's, you can use certain terms and figures that you can't use with a general audience. Be careful to match the level to the audience. Work on breaking down the statistics to numbers that are meaningful to your listeners.

The second point to remember is that while one or two dramatically presented statistics can make your audience sit up and take notice, too many figures can confuse them.

The Torah Thought

We are blessed with a Torah that provides an unending source of thought. Whether you're speaking at a Sheva Brachos, a Bar Mitzvah, a graduation, a ground-breaking, a farewell party, or any other event, the right Torah thought is always in place. Because Judaism is not a religion to be observed only for an hour on Saturday morning, but rather a way of life that encompasses our total being and affects every aspect of life, it is desirable and appropriate always to consider using a *vort*, or a Torah thought. Obviously, it must be appropriate to the occasion and to the audience.

Two important considerations are worth noting: First, you can say a simple *vort!* Perhaps one of the most frequent incidents of a speaker's "abuse" of an audience is that he thinks he must say long or complicated Torah thoughts. If you have been invited to speak to a select group of scholars, a complex, hard-to-follow train of thought may be in place, or even desirable. But for the average audience, a short, simple, clearly explained thought has a better chance of being understood and appreciated.

Let us go one step further. One of our purposes in relating a Torah thought is to endear the Torah and all that it represents to the audience. If we speak about concepts that are not fully explained and which are over the heads of the audience, instead of making the Torah more precious to our listeners, we are using the Torah to insult them. They may "hear" us saying, "You're not learned…" People who have sat through inappropriate, long-winded Torah discussions that were over their heads have said the speakers were condescending and that they felt put down.

As you prepare for a speech, give careful consideration to the choice of your Torah thought. Ask yourself: "Will the audience understand it the way I present it? Can I simplify it? Can I leave out part of it so that it will be easier to understand? Can I add an example to present my point more clearly?"

The second important consideration is that you can say a short *vort*. Ranking close behind the complicated presentation is the mistaken belief that a Torah thought needs to be long. There are Torah thoughts that do require fifteen to twenty minutes of explanation, but there are also thousands of Torah thoughts that only need five minutes, and some that need only two or three minutes! If you have reason to believe that the audience may listen to a four-minute thought but will not listen to a twenty-minute address, why subject them to something that has so little chance of being heard?

Don't crowd a twenty-minute thought into four minutes. It can cause mental indigestion. Don't expand a four-minute thought to twenty minutes. It can cause mental stagnation.

Clearly Define Terms for Your Audience

Do they all understand the *possuk*, the Torah quote? If there is an appreciable number of people in the audience who might not fully understand the Hebrew *possuk*, you should translate it word by word or phrase by phrase into English. At the very least, you should convey the intent of the *possuk* in a sentence or two.

Quote Accurately

This statement sounds fundamental and simple, yet it is often overlooked. Even if you know the *possuk* or *ma'amar Chazal* by heart, take the trouble to look it up in its source. Don't rely on a reference from another *sefer*. Take the time and go directly to the source to look up the original. (Noted speaker Rabbi Paysach Krohn tells his audience the exact *perek* and *possuk* or *blatt* he is citing, so they can easily look it up.)

Practice Reading the Quote Grammatically Correctly

If you don't read the quote grammatically correctly, you run the risk of allowing the wrong pronunciation to block out the thought you're trying to convey to your audience. Some people in your audience won't hear or remember the beautiful thought, only the mistake! When you quote during a speech, you're always open to being corrected (in public!), an embarrassment you really don't need. So practice reading your material correctly. If you have difficulty, ask an expert how he reads it and learn how to pronounce it correctly.

And by all means, write down the quote with *nekudos*! Whether or not you will be able to repeat it from memory, have the quote clearly written with *nekudos*.

Review the Major Meforshim

In reviewing the major commentaries, you may be embarrassed to find that you misunderstood the *possuk*, and therefore decide not to use it. Or you may discover that a major commentary gives a totally different or opposite meaning to the one in the source you want to quote. You may yet decide to use the *vort*, but never be taken by surprise. Know in advance what the major *meforshim* say about the subject. You owe it to your audience to first present the accepted interpretation before introducing the innovative thought.

Chapter Six
VERBAL AND
NON-VERBAL MESSAGES

Watch Your Words

*T*he same thought said one way, using one group of words, can endear you to your listeners; yet another group of words, which may sound similar to the casual listener, can send an entirely different message. Instead of endearment, it can elicit resentment.

Here is a simple example: You want to present something difficult and would like to urge your audience to listen more carefully. Notice the different nuances in the following sentences.

"This material is hard and requires your full attention."

"You will not understand it unless you listen carefully."

"Other audiences have asked me to go over this material slowly, so please listen carefully."

"The material is seemingly easy; but audiences have told me that until they heard it twice, they didn't understand. You look like a bright group — if we listen carefully, we should understand it the first time."

When you practice your speech, listen to your choice of words. In any sensitive areas discuss the choice of words with a knowledgeable confidant.

Keep It Simple

Listening to a speech usually means keeping all the information you hear in your mind. In a book, you can read a sentence and refer back to it; however, when you speak, your audience has to keep that sentence in their minds.

For example: Suppose I want to tell you that two words have the same *shoresh* (Hebrew root). If I were writing this in a book, I could place both words next to each other, or on consecutive lines, and my point would be clearly understood by any reader. As a classroom teacher, I can use the blackboard to make the same point.

However, if I am a speaker, I am asking my audience to visualize the words, to hold in their minds one word and to compare it to a second word. Keeping two phrases in your mind for the purpose of comparison may not be a large assignment; yet surprisingly, even this simple request will lose a few people in your audience.

As you expand the material that has to be remembered to three or four phrases, a few sentences, or a long list of numbers, you progressively keep losing more of your audience. As a speaker, you must be extremely sensitive to what you're asking the audience to do. You may find it advisable to use a visual aid, a card or board to help you get your point across; you may decide to change the thrust of your speech to make it more easily understood; or you may decide to simplify your presentation with an example to help the audience understand and remember a complicated concept.

A friend of mine had to make a presentation to a board of directors to advocate funding for a project. He had prepared a long speech and numerous fact sheets with figures to prove his point. A few days before the meeting, he learned that he was to be the fifth speaker. He recalled that he had heard a funny story that capsulized the very point he wanted to make in his speech. He decided to walk in, tell the story and then distribute just one fact sheet containing just the most important figures.

He came into the meeting, told his story, distributed his fact sheet and carried the day. The funny story made the presentation for him. It was refreshingly simple and to the point, in contrast to the rambling, fact-laden presentations that suffered from overload.

Of course, figures are important, and there is a place for long, complicated explanations, but consider your audience carefully.

Speaker to Listener = Original to Fax

Compare the communication process that takes place in public speaking to the communication process involved in sending a fax. The fax machine allows a person to send a copy of what is on a sheet of paper to a similar machine in just a few seconds. You can put down on paper words, figures, drawings, music, algebraic equations, foreign languages — anything – and transmit it to another machine down the block, across town, in another city, over the ocean. If your machine and the receiving machine are both in working order, the recipient should get exactly what you sent.

However, if your original is blurred, smudged, or chopped off at the ends, then the fax received can be no better; in fact, it could be considerably worse.

How similar that is to speaking in public! If your presentation is poorly structured, then your audience's "copy" will be blurred. If your speech is choppy with incomplete thoughts and examples not fully developed, your audience's understanding will be no better. If your original is weak — without enthusiasm or excitement, filled with bland, colorless, nondescript words — then your audience's copy can't be much better. What you put in is the best you can hope to get out.

When you feel simplicity and directness would be of greater value, don't hesitate to use them.

If you try to make your speech uncomplicated, shorten it, simplify it, and break it into easier ideas, it will be long remembered.

Six Messages We Want To Send Our Audience (Without Saying So)

As the audience settles back to listen to your opening remarks, there are many thoughts going through their minds. Even if the introduction gave information about who you are and why you earned the right to speak, there are still questions about you and the quality of your speaking ability. If you address these properly, you will put the audience at ease, and they will listen more attentively.

1. I am well prepared.

The audience is not interested in how long you prepared, to whom you spoke, or where you got your message, no more than you are when you are a guest in a restaurant and have no interest in the problems the chef encountered in preparing the meal. But they do want to be reassured that you have done your homework.

A woman who lived in a large mid-western city told me that every year her organization would fly in a guest speaker and pay a considerable honorarium. Invariably the speaker would begin by saying, "On the plane it occurred to me..." or "While traveling here today, I thought of..." The chairlady was justifiably per-turbed because they had engaged the speaker many weeks in advance, and yet the subtle message was, "I began preparing my speech today on the flight over here!" (The reason the speaker used that opening was to convey a sense of creativity and fresh-ness, but the negative impact was not considered. Perhaps what could have been said was, "In reviewing my notes on the plane today, I thought of this point." Now we have conveyed both points: freshness and a sense of preparation.)

You don't necessarily have to verbalize the answers to each of the audience's mental questions. Perhaps once you are aware of your audience's desire to know the answers, the way you give your speech will answer the questions. For example, "I am pre-pared" might be projected by the way you stand at the podium, the organization of your notes, or the few words on a flip chart. "I am sensitive to time" can be projected by having the chair-person introduce you as a speaker who knows how to start and end on time, or by insisting that the speech start on time.

To demonstrate preparedness, you may want to use some of these as inserts in your speech:

- ▸ I have had an opportunity to do some research on our topic...
- ▸ To get some background on our topic, I spoke to six manufacturers...
- ▸ You may be interested in knowing that twenty-nine books were published in the last three years on this subject. While I didn't read all of them, I did get a good idea of their content...

2. I am organized.

Preparation means having much information. Organization means having this information in order of importance, knowing what to say (and what to leave out), and knowing when to say it. If you don't have a clearly defined objective, if you don't know exactly what message you want to leave with your audience, your speech will be nothing more than a smorgasbord of ideas and facts. You don't want to offer just a smorgasbord: on the contrary, you want to serve a five-course meal. Course one is an entree, then salad and soup, followed by the main dish and topped by dessert. The guests at such a meal know that the chef not only prepared food, he coordinated it so that it would be served to everyone's utmost enjoyment. As soon as you walk into a banquet, you know whether the meal is a smorgasbord or whether it will be served.

In the same way, the audience wants to be assured that you will serve ideas in a coordinated way. There are numerous ways we can send this message. We can say, "There are six points I want to make." That says in a simple way that you have an outline that you will follow. Any statement that indicates you plan to follow an outline signals that your speech is organized. Here are some additional openings:

- ▸ We can divide our subject into four segments...
- ▸ Just remember one word and you'll remember each point. The word is "Leader." The "L" can remind us of...
- ▸ I have carefully organized my presentation so you can easily remember it...

3. I understand you.

One of the barriers that separate speaker and audience is the gap of economic, social, religious, cultural, or political differences. For example, if a banker who earns several million dollars a year is speaking to a group of factory workers earning $30,000 a year, the audience would have reason to question whether the speaker could relate to them. Until this question is answered in the audience's minds, every statement that the banker makes will be suspect and held up to the question: "Does he really understand my economic position?"

The urgency of answering this question is dependent on the subject of the speech. If the audience members are photographers and the speech is about a new method of photography, the economic gap is less important. If the subject is "How to Prepare for Retirement," the economic difference is probably uppermost in everyone's mind and should be addressed at the outset.

The audience has to get a feeling that even if the speaker lives in a different world, he understands them nevertheless. This understanding can come from many sources: personal experience, the experiences of close friends, travel or reading. Phrases like these make this clear:

▸ In my youth I spent three years working in a factory...
▸ In my travels I often spent time learning about...
▸ My family came from...
▸ To get a better appreciation of you, my audience, I...

> ▸ My father never earned more than $10,000 a year: I know firsthand the problems you are experiencing...

4. I am sensitive to time, both yours and mine.

If you ask a hundred people what they most dislike about public speakers, the vast majority of them will say, "They talk too long!" Speakers easily fall in love with the sound of their own voices. They think of every phrase as the world's greatest poetic expression. They aren't willing to spend the time and effort to trim all the fat. It is much easier to talk and talk than it is to sharpen the thought. It is easier to include all the stories and jokes than it is to carefully and critically evaluate which to include and which to leave out.

The audience wants to hear a subtle signal from you that you are different. Not only are you prepared and organized, you have pared the fat, eliminated the unnecessary and will deliver in the shortest time possible a succinct presentation. Use expressions like these:

> ▸ In the twelve minutes allotted to me...
> ▸ Because I want to pack a lot of information into just a few minutes...
> ▸ To make the most effective use of our time together, I have boiled down our subject...

5. I am enthusiastic about my speech.

It has been said that there is no such thing as a boring subject, just boring speakers. The proof is that you can find people who are enthusiastic about subjects many of us would find uninteresting. Speak to a person who has spent a lifetime collecting stamps and you'll be overwhelmed by his excitement about the subject. Just ask a few leading questions and you'll have difficulty stopping the flood of information, facts, and figures.

Whatever topic you choose to speak about, the audience has a right to be caught up in your excitement and enthusiasm.

6. I know when to stop.

Have you ever been on an airplane that begins to descend and then the pilot begins circling the airport? That is how an audience feels when a speaker begins to end his speech, but changes his mind. He adds just one more thought or one more story, and goes into a "holding pattern," to the frustration and dismay of the audience.

The audience has the right to be assured that after you have prepared, organized, cut the fat, and delivered an enthusiastic presentation, you know not only when to finish, but how to end your speech smoothly.

The Unspoken Message

From your manner, tone and organized presentation, you want your audience to infer several things about you:

I am well prepared.

I am organized.

I understand you.

I am sensitive to time, both yours and mine.

I am enthusiastic about my speech.

I know when to stop.

Podium: Friend or Foe?

If used incorrectly, the podium or speaker's lectern can be perceived by the audience as a barrier put there to hide you, or as a crutch to support you if you faint. The real purpose of a lectern is to provide a place for notes and to position you properly for the microphone.

Since so much of the impact of a speaker is visual, experts say that more than fifty percent of you should be totally visible. In fact, you would be most effective if you stood where the audience can see you — no podium, no table, just you. With no barrier at all, your total body language, how you stand, the use of your hands and arms, the few steps that you take to come closer to the audience, will reinforce the points you make in your speech.

In practice, we use a lectern to hold some notes. But don't hide behind it. Here are some helpful suggestions:

- Try to get the smallest, least obstructive lectern.
- Walk from behind the podium to stand next to it. Plan several places in your speech where you want to get "closer" to your audience or use your full body to emphasize a point.
- Be aware that a stage that puts you several feet above the floor level of the audience suggests that you are on a "higher level" than they are.

Obviously, the size and configuration of the room may require that you speak from a stage. However, I have seen many cases in which the chairman of the event took it for granted that the speaker would prefer a stage, even when there was no real reason for it.

I remember one speaker who was asked to address a small group. He insisted that the podium be removed from the stage and placed at floor level. He also refused to use the microphone, indicating that his audience was really a group of friends and that he would like to address them as friends. Even before he began his presentation, he earned the strong appreciation of every person in the room.

- ▸ Don't "white-knuckle" the podium. Hanging on to the lectern for dear life is perceived by the audience as a sign of insecurity.
- ▸ Don't pace, shake, move back and forth, or simulate a ping-pong ball. While it is true that the audience wants to see you in action, to feel your excitement and enthusiasm and to see full body movements, you should not carry this to the point of distraction.

If you do any motion at the lectern that calls attention to itself it pulls attention away from your speech. So we really need to be sensitive to a fine line.

We do want movement. We do want life, we want action, vigor, and vitality, but we want these actions to be smoothly done so that they do not call attention to themselves. Walking away from the podium and taking a few steps into the aisle where the audience is sitting sends a powerful message that "I am one of you," but do that several times, and it will be seen as a cheap, annoying gimmick.

The next few time you attend a speech, take special notice of where the speakers stand. If you can find the opportunity to sit in several seats — up front, at an extreme side of the room, in the last row — and see how the occupants of these seats view the speaker, you'll become sensitive as to the best position to take when you speak.

Chapter Seven

TIPS ON PRESENTATION

How to Dress for a Speech

*A*s intelligent people, we would like to think that the content of a speech is the only important element and that the "package" is not important. Yet the person who says, "You don't sell a book by its cover" has never tried to sell books, because in fact, we do judge a book by its cover! We look at the cover to decide whether we want to pick it up to read. Likewise, we do evaluate if we want to listen to a speech by the way the speaker looks.

How you dress becomes a major factor contributing to this impression. There are two more reasons why you should "dress up" to speak. The first is to honor the audience. If this speech is important — and every speech should be important; if you value the audience — and every audience should be valued, then your dress should indicate that fact.

Dress is one of the ways we signal what level of importance we attach to any situation. You wear one set of clothing to work around the yard or to move furniture; you wear a different set of clothing when you attend a wedding, because what you wear conveys the importance of an occasion. Your audience will feel flattered that you have "dressed up" for the speech. It reflects your opinion of them, and the better they perceive that opinion, the more chance you have of being listened to.

The second reason to dress up is for you yourself. People tend to do better when they feel better about themselves, and dressing up definitely is one way of feeling better about oneself.

Obviously "dressing up," means that you dress in good taste. You don't want to call attention to your clothing just to create a perception of being well dressed. Wearing a tuxedo when everyone else is wearing a suit would call attention to yourself and draw it away from your speech.

The speaker who is well put-together, whose clothing is properly pressed, shoes shined, who is well groomed, has a greater chance of holding the audience's attention.

You may occasionally see a successful speaker in his shirtsleeves or dressed sloppily, but wouldn't he be better respected and more successful if he didn't look sloppy? Why have anything that you can control work against you? Your clothing and your grooming are easily in your control: use them to your advantage.

Just Before You Speak

The wrong way: The ride to the hall usually takes half an hour, so you leave at 7:15 for your eight o'clock speech. Five minutes of extra traffic and one wrong turn brings you to the hall at 7:55. You have never been to this room before. You walk into the hall, and before you have a chance to catch your breath, you're "on." If you think that's a ridiculous exaggeration, you'd be surprised how many times I have actually seen that happen, especially when the speaker flies in from another city.

The right way:

> 1. See the room in which you will speak in advance. If it is local and you have never been there before, perhaps you can drive over a few days before your speaking engagement. Where will you park? What is the best entrance? How do you get to the room? Where will the dais be? Are there steps up to the speaking platform? (The best speech will not be effective if you fall on your face going up to or coming down from the platform!) What lights will be on and off?

> What you want to do in advance of your speech is to get a "feel" for the room. You want to stand at the podium and become acquainted with the territory. You want to change the room from a large, cold, intimidating stranger to a warm friend. If you stand at the podium for a few minutes in the empty room, you'll begin to chip away at the intimidation. If you can say the first few sentences of your speech to the empty hall, if you can practice walking from

your seat to the lectern and back, you'll familiarize yourself with the logistics and you'll help chip away at your fear.

One of the elements of fear is doing something new. As soon as you have done it several times, it isn't new anymore. (There are, of course, many ingredients to fear, but if you can minimize even one by this method, it is to your advantage to do it.)

Walk around the room to the furthest point away from the head table. Sit in the furthest seats. Sit in the seats in the middle of the room. Make the room "your place," and when the big moment comes, you'll feel more comfortable.

If you travel a long distance to your speaking engagement, you may want to be taken from the airport directly to the hall for a few minutes, just to be able to acquaint yourself with it. After that you can go to your hotel or motel for a short rest, shower, and final preparation.

2. The hour before you speak is an especially important time for you to get into and remain in an upbeat, positive and inspirational frame of mind. It is not the time to eat heavy food. Digestion will put demands on your body for more blood, taking it away from your brain. It is also not the time to drink alcoholic beverages or to be involved in heavy or confrontational conversation.

3. Have your notes in your suit pocket or purse, and a photocopy in another pocket or elsewhere. This will provide an extra sense of protection. Don't leave your notes on the lectern; the chairman or someone else can mistakenly walk off with them.

4. Many speakers have found that a few minutes of light exercise or a short walk will make them feel a little sharper. Even three minutes of deeply breathing fresh air will do wonders.

5. A quick visit to the restroom, a careful, detailed viewing in a full-length mirror, and now you're ready to share your thoughts with a group of friends in a familiar place.

You may not always be able to do all of these preparations, but it is to your advantage to have this checklist of suggestions and to check off as many as you can.

To be effective, you must be comfortable with your material, with your audience and with yourself!

Overcoming Nervousness

Logically, any person who can physically speak the language and can communicate to one person should have no trouble addressing ten or a hundred people. In reality, speaking in public has always been associated with fear. Even the Talmud uses the expression "fear of the public."

This fear is not imagined; it is real and expressed by sweaty palms, knotted stomach, tight throat, shaking knees — all symptoms of actual fear.

While there is no magic formula or pill to eliminate fear of public speaking, there are ways to chip away at it slowly, and eventually to overcome the fear factor.

In the professional public speaking industry, there is a saying: "The objective is not to get rid of the butterflies in your stomach. What you want to do is to get the butterflies to fly in formation."

How do you overcome fear? The steps are simple, if not easy.

1. You're well prepared. You have done your homework well. You have become an "expert" on the subject at hand.

2. You have done "private thinking." You acquired information, did your research and then did your own thinking. You spoke to people who have the opposite view. You have crystallized your ideas. In short, the material is now "yours."

3. You have practiced. You have repeated the main part of your presentation a number of times to good friends who have told you that it is good! If possible, you have practiced in a large, empty hall.

To appreciate this last point — practicing in a large, empty hall — consider the following scenario. You are asked to speak to a group of twenty people in a small meeting room. After you have written your speech, you choose to practice it in a five-hundred-seat auditorium. You practice fifteen times in this large, empty room, using no microphone, but speaking as loudly as you can. Although the auditorium was empty when you practiced, the confidence that you have developed by standing on a stage and projecting your voice will make the small meeting room seem shrunken and dwarfed by comparison, and the twenty people will not seem as intimidating.

4. You are physically, mentally, and emotionally in top form. You're rested, showered, elegantly dressed; you're relaxed, you're ready.

5. You believe you can do it. Others less capable than you have done it. You're prepared: you can and will do it too.

Even experienced speakers tell of an anxiety or burst of nervous energy that they feel before a speech, but they view this as a positive force. They want to start a speech with an excitement and a visible enthusiasm. Some nervousness is a valuable ally.

Don't Put Yourself Down

Here is an interesting question: Does the audience want you to succeed in your speech? I contend that they do, and here are the reasons:

Firstly, there is a general feeling of empathy with a speaker. The audience knows only too well how uncomfortable they would be if they had to speak in public (that's why so few people do), and generally they respect and admire you for doing what they can't do. This respect and admiration will last until you give them a reason to believe otherwise.

The second reason the audience wants you to do well is a personal one; they want to justify their investment in coming to hear you speak. Every member of the audience has invested his time, and often his money, to hear you speak. He has given up an hour or two to attend the affair where you're speaking. Perhaps he has also invested money to purchase a ticket, buy a journal ad, pay for a baby sitter, or traveled a distance to be there. When you speak well, you validate his good judgment! You show him that he was right to expend time and money.

If you don't speak well, then he was wrong in making the investment. Human nature is such that most of us want to be right all the time. Therefore, until you do something to signal otherwise, the audience will be on your side.

When you fully understand this point, you'll realize that any self-deprecating statement is counterproductive. The audience wants you to be a winner, they want to hear a professional, and if you are self-deprecating, you are ruining their expectations.

If you tell your audience that you are unprepared, if you apologize, if you suggest that you did not do your homework, you are really saying, "Folks, I'm sorry that I am not the real pro you thought I was!" You have informed them that they were wrong in their choice of a speaker, wrong in their investment of time and money to come listen to you. You have effectively changed a friend into an opponent, a supporter into an antagonist. My advice to the speaker is to ride the crest of the audience's good wishes. Indicate to the audience that you did prepare, because they are so important to you! Confirm their belief that you're a pro, and they'll listen to you.

Self-deprecating statements are counterproductive. The audience wants you to be a winner!

We're Looking At You!

Long before you begin your official speech, the audience is trying to get answers to their questions about you. They want to know what type of person you are, whether you are friendly, courteous, really interested in their cause, gracious. From the moment that you come into the audience's view, you're on display. If you're a guest speaker at a banquet and you join the guests at the meal, the audience will carefully observe the way you stand (upright, with good posture, or drooping), the way you sit (interested, alert, or disinterested), the way you speak at the table (whether you are soft, smiling, or argumentative). All these will help the audience evaluate you.

If you're the third speaker and you have a bored look on your face during the presentations of the first two speakers, you are making a clear statement that you have no real interest in the program or organization, that you just want to get it over with and leave. That message will not endear you to your audience.

The message you want to project is that you are a bright, polite, concerned person who is pleased to be at this affair, and that you have an exciting and interesting message to share.

Moving an audience from a position of neutral interest to one of positive interest is a hard enough task for any public speaker. Why make it even more difficult for yourself by giving the audience reason to dislike you?

Put your best foot forward and they'll be on your side.

Chapter Eight

INTRODUCTIONS: HOW TO MAKE THEM AND HOW TO SURVIVE THEM

When You Are the Chairman

*I*f you are called upon to be chairman of an event, you should view your first task as introducing the guests, welcoming them, and making them feel comfortable. You may want to express some thoughts about the purpose of the affair and set the tone. This should take four to six minutes. After you have done this, you then come to the second part, which is to introduce the first speaker with a brief introduction. Two to three minutes should suffice in almost all situations. Longer than three minutes puts the audience (and the speaker) on edge. It may become counterproductive, with the audience thinking, "If he's so good, let's hear him already."

In addition, an overdone introduction does not flatter the speaker or the audience. It sets the speaker up for an impossible task ("He is the funniest person you ever heard!") and it insults the audience. ("Does the chairman really think that we are so gullible that we believe that?")

The chairman who abuses the podium by speaking for fifteen or twenty minutes sends a message to all the speakers which says, "Forget about any time constrictions; you can talk as long as you want!" It is the chairman's primary obligation to see to it that the program moves, that speakers, dedications and entertainment all flow. If he sets the wrong example by speaking too long, he can't expect other speakers to keep to their allotted times.

Much of the success or failure of a program depends on timing. Caterers, waiters and entertainers are all thrown off schedule and out of kilter because of poor timing, resulting in a program that pleases no one. Therefore, a chairman has to be sure to insist on accurate time limits for the speakers, and then set the example himself.

How to Make an Introduction

To the surprise of many people, the real purpose of an introduction is not to sneak in an additional guest speaker! The purpose of an introduction is to answer the unasked questions of the audience:

1. Who is this speaker?

2. What has he done that should interest me?

3. Why should I listen to him?

Depending on the situation, there may be even more such questions.

Theoretically, a speaker could answer these questions himself at the beginning of his speech. He could say, "My name is Rabbi Plony Almony, I live in Chicago, and I'm a rabbi at the Lakeshore Day School, which I started in 1975. I have an interesting presentation that will stimulate your thinking..." But most speakers would feel awkward conveying this information about themselves, and the audience would likewise feel uncomfortable listening to a person speak about himself.

Just as common courtesy dictates that you introduce two friends who have never met each other, common courtesy has created the procedure of introducing a speaker.

If you are the chairman of the evening, you perform the function of introducing two people whom you know, the speaker and each member of the audience. Imagine that you are the chairman of a charity banquet in Los Angeles, and the guest speaker is a friend with whom you worked closely in an identical organization in New York. You respect him for his dedication to the cause and his leadership qualities. As chairman, this is the message you want to get across to the audience: "This man has hands-on experience that can help us; he is a genuine, devoted person. He is successful in his own business, and he is an inspirational leader. Let's listen to him."

If you met some friends and the guest speaker in the hall before the dinner, that's probably what you would say to them by way of introduction. That's the flow of what you want to say now from the podium.

What you want to do is help your friend jump-start his speech. You want him to talk to an audience who is already warmed up to him. You want your friends in the audience to listen to a mutual friend. He's not a stranger. You want to build a bridge of trust between speaker and audience, as if to say, "Believe me, I know him, and he is good. Trust me, and give him your attention!"

Because introductions are abused so often, I want to give you one more example, even at the risk of belaboring the point. Imagine that you are a salesman and arrive for an appointment with a prospective client. Before you even have a chance to say anything, he says to you, "My best friend Joe Joseph told me all about you. He said you are scrupulously honest, have quality merchandise and fair prices, and that I'll greatly enjoy doing business with you!" You're going to do very well because your prospect is pre-sold, and you're coming in on second base. You're not just a salesman — you're a friend's friend.

Compare that scenario to a prospective client who sits behind his desk, hands folded across his chest, and says, " I don't know who you are, I don't know why you're here and I don't know your company. I don't know why I should trust you. Now talk to me!"

The purpose of an introduction is to turn the speaker into a friend of the audience, a person to whom they will listen and whom they will believe. The speaker now has to maintain the momentum. He has to build on the chairman's projection of friendship, and he has to live up to the expectation of the audience. A poor speech will fail regardless of how well it is introduced, but we want to help launch it as best we can. Likewise, a really good speaker will survive and do well even after a bad introduction, but why start with a strike against you?

Elements of the Introduction

If you, as the chairman, are to represent the good friend of the speaker, you should know something about him. Here are the elements to consider in an introduction: the full name of the speaker, his title, current position, major accomplishments (if they are relevant), and possibly a story that would endear him to the audience.

Name of speaker: Let's make sure of the name he wants used. Is it Jacob, Yaakov, or Jake? Does he use his middle name? Is he

Yaakov Shmuel, Jacob Samuel, Jake, Sammy? Find out the correct pronunciation of his name as well.

Title: How does he want to be introduced — as Jacob Silversmith, as Mr. Jacob Silversmith, or as Rabbi Jacob Silversmith?

Current position: Your audience probably wants to know what he does for a living. The answer should almost always come from the speaker. You would want to ask him, "How do you want to be introduced?" If the title by itself does not convey the grandeur of his office, you may want to expand on it. For example, "Rabbi of Northshore Synagogue" doesn't say much. You may want to add that he built the synagogue in ten years from twenty families to three hundred families.

Major accomplishments: Did he write a book relevant to the speech he is going to give? Did he lead, organize, or represent something that the audience knows about? When the audience is familiar with his cause, they'll feel closer to him, or at least more receptive to his speech. Can you put these facts into your introduction in just a few words?

What we don't want is a long list of titles and accomplishments that are not relevant, but only sound good. You may want to add one or two sentences about what the speaker will say in his speech, if — and this is a big "if" — the additions will further interest the audience without giving away his speech.

I was told about a speaker who, in casual discussion with the chairman, told him the three or four main points he intended to make in his speech. The chairman, in his eagerness to excite the audience, got carried away and said, "We will have a wonderful speech by our guest speaker. He will tell us..." Then he went on to enumerate the key points! When he was done, the speaker had lost his thunder and had no enthusiasm left for the speech.

Your introduction should build a bridge of friendship between the audience and the speaker, answering the audience's unexpressed questions. Do all this in two minutes, and let the speaker shine.
Both speaker and audience will appreciate your kindness!

How to Survive an Introduction

The simplest piece of advice is not to allow the chairman to wing it, but to help him by providing him with a typed introduction for him to read.

Many people feel this advice is immodest, and they are uncomfortable with it. ("Doesn't it look presumptuous of me to write my own introduction?") After you have suffered through several well-intended, but ridiculous, introductions, that have your occupation, accomplishments, title and name wrong, you'll appreciate the professional way in which your own introduction does the job.

Your introduction could also be tailored to set the mood you plan to evoke in your speech. You would be surprised at how many seemingly off-the-cuff words of the chairman were actually very carefully worded by the speaker. The name of the game is effectiveness, smooth transitions and perceptions of professionalism. The audience would rather you write the introduction and provide them with one that is smooth and flowing than to witness the fumbling of a chairman who doesn't know anything about you and is groping for words.

Chapter Nine

IMPROVING YOUR SKILLS

Using a TAGI Sheet

*O*ne of the ways we can grow in our profession is by getting feedback. If we can find out the truthful assessment of what went over well and what didn't, in essence how effective we were, we can try to repeat what went well and improve what didn't.

Added advantages:

1. You can collect names and addresses (of potential buyers or people interested in your cause).

2. You can collect positive statements you may want to use in your future advertising.

3. You can learn interesting things about yourself and the audience from the comments.

4. The sheet indicates that you're a real professional who wants to improve. What a nice statement about you!

Several years ago, I devised a hand-out sheet to encourage audiences to listen carefully and take notes. I call it TAGI, which is an abbreviation of That's A Good Idea! At the bottom of the sheet is a tear-off evaluation form to furnish you with the desired feedback. After your speech, you can have the tear-off collected while the audience takes home their list of Good Ideas. (If you can't arrange to print a sheet with a perforated tear-off section at the bottom, you can use two sheets of paper and have the audience hand in the second sheet to you.)

When handing out the sheet, you may want to introduce it in this way:

"Before we begin, I would like to introduce this TAGI sheet. 'TAGI', as you will note at the top of the sheet itself, stands for 'That's A Good Idea.' It serves four purposes:

> 1. It encourages you to take notes.
>
> 2. The tear-off sheet at the bottom gives you an opportunity to express your comments, evaluation, questions, and suggestions. Each comment will be read.
>
> 3. You can evaluate this session on the tear-off sheet. Please indicate how effective you thought this speech was and your level of enjoyment.
>
> 4. If you care to write your name and address, you will receive some follow-up information.

At the end of this session, please hand the tear-off sheet to an usher."

A sample TAGI sheet is on the following pages. Obviously it can only be used in a lecture or workshop situation, but consider it an example of a feedback attempt.

Note: Experience teaches us that most people who choose to complete the TAGI sheet evaluation section will overrate the speaker, so enjoy the high ratings, but don't let them go to your head!

Let's Share Ideas *The purpose of our time together is to share ideas.* Ideas that stimulate new thinking, reinforce old thinking, clarify cloudy thinking (it may even provoke you to disagree and substitute your own thinking). Ideas that are simple, direct and practical. Ideas that you could put to immediate use.

Because our minds think so quickly, we can be exposed to a new idea, think about it for an instant, and within a few seconds, lose it. We can listen to a speech or lecture, hear some wonderful suggestions, even be inspired… and go home with nothing. There is a better more effective way and it's called "aggressive listening."

Aggressive Listening The hallmark of an "aggressive listener" is the attitude:

"I am investing my valuable time and do not want to lose even one good idea. I will listen with an open mind, grasp onto every idea that I can use, **write it down** *and then have it ready to put into action. Because I will use a scoop, not a sieve, I hope to come home with a "bucket of ideas."*

I would be honored if you would take home even one or two ideas to use, so that our time together will have been well spent. Please write your ideas on this sheet.

At the conclusion of our session, please complete the tear off sheet and hand it to the usher to receive a free follow-up. Thank you.

(Your name here.)

Please hand this tear-off sheet to usher at end of session.

Evaluation (Optional)

On a scale of 1-10 (1 being the least) score: Effectiveness _____ Enjoyment _____

❏ Please mail follow-up

Name_____

Address_____

City / State / Zip_____

Please share your comments, evaluations, questions and suggestions on the reverse side.

TAGI*
notes

***T**hat's **A** **G**ood **I**dea

Stimulating Your Ideas and Creative Thoughts

The purpose of this form is to challenge you to think through each element of your speech and to find methods of improving them. To benefit from this exercise, you need an open mind, the courage to think of new ideas, and/or a new way to present your material.

Try to consider several different ways to open a speech so that you can choose the best, most effective opening. Don't become a "one-method" speaker! For example, if you usually ask a question to open a speech, now consider the other alternatives. You may be pleasantly surprised to find a better way to achieve your objective.

Instead of trying to just answer the following questions, allow the questions to stimulate new thoughts.

1. Have I earned the right to speak?

> How can I learn more about the subject?
>
> Read: newspapers, magazines, books, speeches, trade sources, other _____
>
> Speak: to co-workers, employees, employers, buyers, customers, users, competition, salesmen, other _____
>
> Listen: to lectures, cassettes, other _____
>
> Visit: stores, plants, sites, conventions, other _____

2. Did the material have time to "percolate"?

　　Have I done my own thinking on it? _____

　　How would I change the situation? _____

　　How can I retain the benefits and eliminate the negatives?

　　_____

　　What new subject, idea, or element can I add or delete to change the concept?_____

　　Do I have my subject clearly defined?_____

　　Have I outlined my material?_____

3. How can I stimulate my thinking?

　　To whom can I present my idea(s) and/or opinion(s) who would (vehemently) disagree? _____

　　What argument can I develop if I had to take the opposite point of view? _____

　　_____

4. In one precise sentence, describe what you want to say.

　　_____

5. List the five strongest key words or phrases that support your position. _____

　　_____

　　_____

　　_____

　　_____

6. Opening: Consider the various ways to open a speech.

    1. Arouse curiosity.

    2. Tell a story.

    3. Give a specific illustration.

    4. Use an exhibit.

    5. Ask a question (or offer a challenge).

    6. Quote.

    7. State a shocking fact.

    8. Use a joke.

    9. Thank your audience.

    10. Other _____

7. Message: How can I bridge the gap between the opening and the message?

    What is the most dramatic point? _____

    What is the most interesting point? _____

    What can I do to make my point more believable? _____

    1. Use testimony.

    2. Use a personal story.

    3. Quote from famous or important people.

    4. Read letters, newspapers, books.

    5. Use a professional source.

    6. Other _____

How can I make my points clearer?

> 1. Use examples.
>
> 2. Use a large display.
>
> 3. Hand out sheets.
>
> 4. Other _____

How can I make the speech more understandable?

> 1. Make the main point several times in different ways.
>
> 2. Give time for the audience to digest the material.
>
> 3. Summarize the material midway through the speech.
>
> 4. Other _____

8. Closing: How can I bridge the gap between the message and the closing?

> How would each of these closings do?
>
> 1. Summary
>
> 2. Appeal for action
>
> 3. Compliment
>
> 4. Quote
>
> 5. Other _____

9. Practice: Did I practice the opening, starting from sitting in my seat, being introduced, walking up to the lectern, and beginning the speech?

> Did I practice handling any exhibits or other material? ____

Do I have a smooth closing? _____

Did I practice walking away and down from the lectern?

_____

Did I time my speech? _____

Did I record the speech and listen to it as objectively as I can? _____

On a scale of one to ten, would I, as a member of the audience, be totally bored (1) or highly interested (10) in my speech? _____

What can I do to increase the interest intensity of my speech? _____

Chapter Ten

YOU: THE PROFESSIONAL SPEAKER

Take Control

*A*s a speaker, you often have much more to say (no pun intended) about the speaking environment than you realize. You can, and should, ask in advance for a number of conditions to be met in order to make your presentation more effective.

Obviously, there will be many times when you cannot ask for changes, but review this list before you agree to speak, and you'll be amazed how often you can control many factors.

1. The size of the room.

The person who has asked you to speak may have no idea what will serve your needs, or their needs, best. In fact, many times no thought is given to the selection of a room; rather, it is taken for granted, because "we always use that room for lectures." As a result, you may find yourself addressing thirty people in a three-hundred-seat auditorium, an invitation to major disaster.

2. The configuration of the room.

Here is a suggestion I learned many years ago that I have used effectively. If you expect between fifty and one hundred people to come to a speech, have chairs prepared for fifty people and provide for an extra fifty folding chairs to be available in the corner. When fifty people occupy fifty chairs, you have a feeling of success: all seats are taken, there is a full house. When fifty people occupy one hundred seats, there is a sense of failure.

You can fill a larger room with fewer chairs by leaving larger aisles between the rows and more space at the front of the room.

3. Get people to fill the front seats first.

You can suggest to the chairman that he cordon off the back seats until all the front seats are full. If all else fails, before you begin, you can ask the people in the back rows to come up front. Realize that most people feel "uncomfortable" up front and tend to gravitate towards the back of the room. They will, however, respond to a gentle, friendly request.

4. Ask that the lights be left on.

Since so much of the impact of a speech is visual, ask that all the house lights be left on. You want the audience to see you. The importance of this will be discussed more fully in the "Lights On" section.

5. Learn how to use the microphone properly.

A microphone can enable people in the back of a large room to hear a speech as clearly as those up front, if (and this is a big "if") it is used properly. While the purpose of a microphone is quite simple — to enable the audience at the far end to hear you — numerous speakers seem to believe that the real purpose of a microphone is to amplify their voice, whether or not it is needed. They mistakenly believe that a microphone is an instrument of power. Realize that a microphone actually is a barrier between you and the audience. When you are speaking to a large crowd, you need it, but when you are speaking to a small group, don't use it. Here are some further points on the use of a microphone:

▸ If at all possible, get into the hall early and speak into the microphone for a few minutes so that you become acquainted with it.

▸ Your mouth should be six to eight inches away from the microphone. Since the sound of your voice will change as you move away from the microphone, be careful not to sway or walk away from the lectern. A hand-held microphone gives you freedom of movement, but it creates an additional distraction. I don't recommend it. If you want to walk away from the lectern, a mike that attaches to your lapel is the best alternative.

▸ Any noise at the lectern will be heard. A whisper, the rustling of paper, the tapping of a pencil, all become terribly disturbing when amplified by a microphone. Be especially careful of a whispered comment. Many speakers have been embarrassed by an offhand comment they thought no one could hear that came over the microphone loud and clear.

6. Check the room temperature.

Speaking to an audience in a hot, stuffy room is a sure way to invite them to sleep. Check the room temperature, and if possible, set it two or three degrees lower than usual.

7. Food control.

Discuss in advance whether food will be served, and/or tables will be cleared while you speak. Urge the chairman to refrain from having food served during your speech.

8. Cameras.

Will pictures be taken while you speak? (See notes in the Speakers Information Questionnaire.)

Don't allow the mike to block your face. The audience wants to see you and your facial expression, not a piece of metal!

Lights On

There are three possible problems that you can have with lights.

▸ Too little light

In some banquet halls, the manager likes to dramatize the speaker by dimming all the lights over the audience and placing a spotlight on the speaker. This is great showmanship, but very difficult for public speaking.

As a speaker, you want to see every member of your audience, all of them, not just the first two rows. Unless the lights over the audience are on brightly, you'll look out onto a faceless sea of bodies.

A large audience adds excitement to a presentation. It increases the flow of adrenalin and challenges you to perform your best. But you have to see the audience to gain those benefits. Moreover, when you see them, you may be able to detect some feedback. Facial expressions or body language may indicate that your speech is too long, the room is too warm, or that there is some other problem. If you can't see your audience, you'll miss these signals.

▸ Too much light

A spotlight at a wrong angle or a video light pointed directly toward you will make it difficult to look out at your audience, and uncomfortably hot.

▸ Not enough light on the podium to read your notes

If there is to be a slide show or video presentation before or after your speech, make sure the electricity for the podium light is left on. As a speaker, you have the right to ask the chairman before the program begins to make sure the lights are used properly.

Using the Speaker's Information Questionnaire

Below is a form you can use. It is to be given to the chairman of the event when you are engaged to speak. As you gain experience as a speaker, you may want to modify this form to suit your personal needs. The first part, the questionnaire, should be returned to you. The second part, the guidelines for the chairman, should be given to him/her on a separate sheet of paper.

(Part One) Speaker's Information Questionnaire

To evaluate how I can best serve your needs, please answer the following:

Name of organization: _____

Date of speech _____ Day of week _____ Time _____

Contact person:_____

Address: _____

Phone number of chairman and at location of event: _____

Who is sponsoring this affair? _____

What is the purpose of the presentation? _____

Is this part of a series? _____

Who else will speak? _____

Will food/drink be served? before _____ after speech _____

What precedes and follows the speaker? _____

Is entertainment planned? If yes, what type? _____

Will there be a charge for attendance?_____

Are there any specific areas to avoid? _____

Audience:

     ❏ Men   ❏ Women

     ❏ Jewish   ❏ Non-Jewish

     ❏ Orthodox ❏ Non-Orthodox

     ❏ Members ❏ Non-Members

Anticipated number_____

Predominant age group _____

The audience will be coming from_____

going to _____ home/work/ another lecture

Describe your "typical" audience in terms of education, mood, political and/or religious leanings: _____

Place that speech will be given: (name, address, room number)

_____

Does the use of the building imply political, religious, or any other affiliation? _____

Please describe the room (size, set up, stage, etc.) _____

Will there be a dais? Who will be seated there?_____

_____

Will there be a microphone?_____ What type? _____

What is the announced time of the affair? _____

For how long do you want me to speak? _____

Who will introduce the speaker? (Please discuss this with me.)

_____

What type of advertising is planned? (Local releases, posters, flyers, mailings. There is a bio/picture available. Please discuss this with me.)_____

Are hand-outs, questions and answers desirable? _____

Accommodations:

   To/from my home, airport _____

   Air travel, hotel _____

   To/from speaking location _____

If there will be any change in schedule, please notify me immediately!

Please mail copies of invitation, advertising and program to:

(Part 2) Guidelines for the Chairman

As a courtesy from one professional to another, the following are some procedures that will benefit both of us:

Set-up: I like to be at the area where I will be speaking at least an hour beforehand so I can set up and test the sound system. If another meeting is going on at that time, we can let this go, but where possible, I need to be in the room early to prepare myself.

Introduction: Nothing ruins a good presentation or wastes more valuable time than someone who overdoes the introduction. Enclosed is a brief introduction. Please have the chairman read it, as is.

Sound: Make sure that a good sound system is available and in good working order. I prefer a microphone that attaches to the lapel, if possible.

Food Control: I will not speak while food is being served, eaten, or cleaned up. I expect the service people to wait until my presentation is over to begin clearing the tables. Please keep the kitchen noise down until my presentation is completed.

Audience: I ask you to please be sure that the audience is seated and quiet before I start.

Camera/Publicity: Photographers standing during my presentation, snapping pictures and flashing lights, will be extremely distracting to me. Please keep photography to a minimum. Preferably, I would be happy to have pictures taken before or after the event. Kindly speak to me in advance about arranging this.

Teaching Communication Skills to Children and Students

Speaking clearly, concisely and effectively is one of most desirable skills that a student can learn. This skill, effective public speaking, will enable the child – then the young adult, and eventually the adult – to feel comfortable in communicating ideas one to one or to a group. What is the best advice I can offer on how to teach students public speaking?

First of all, don't make a big deal about it. If we announce to the class that every student will be required to give a "speech," and insist that each student stand at a lectern in front of the class, we will foster the fear and inhibitions most adults have which most children don't have — but can readily learn.

If, however, we begin by casually asking students to recite something sitting in their seats, or standing in place, we will make the process something that is natural.

If we then have students advance to the front of the class and give a simple 2-minute talk or Torah *vort* each week for 20-30 weeks, almost every student will acquire the ability to feel comfortable speaking in public. I know this to be a fact because I often ask good speakers how they learned to project so well, and I often hear the answer, "My grade school teacher had me speak every week."

The second point is: Don't criticize. These two words may be simple to say, but for a teacher who strives for perfection, not to criticize may be a great challenge.

One of the major difficulties in learning how to speak in public is putting one's ego on the line. You expose your thoughts to a roomful of people, each of whom can put you down in many ways. Every member of the audience is capable of overtly (and covertly) laughing at something you said, the way you said it, or something you did standing at the lectern. Whether or not anyone actually laughs at something you say is irrelevant. Just the possibility of someone laughing is enough to make public speaking something most people would rather avoid.

Teacher criticism can cut through a student to his core, and torpedo his self-confidence. Your suggestions can improve his presentation by two percent, but you risk destroying his self-confidence by fifty percent!

Can your students learn without critique? Surprisingly, the answer is yes, if you role model the correct way to address an audience and occasionally mention some ways to improve these skills.

You'll be gratified when a parent tells you, "She expresses herself so clearly now!" or, "My child spoke about the *parshah* so well last Shabbos!"

In fact, the weekly *parshah* offers us an ideal opportunity to convey small, short, self-contained "gems" of thought that the students can use as speeches. You'll enjoy the process and the result.

To parents, I suggest you urge each child to say an easy simple *vort* at the Shabbos table, and do not criticize. When children feel comfortable and secure, they will eventually break through the barrier and learn to express themselves clearly and effectively.

Thirteen Key Points
for Effective Public Speaking

As I stated in the dedication of this book, Rabbi Moshe Sherer, *zt"l*, was a gifted speaker who enthusiastically shared his secrets for success in public speaking. When teaching this special skill, Rabbi Sherer would list for his students Thirteen Key Points to remember when making their presentations. We can still learn these from him.

1. Be brief.

2. Proper gestures are necessary. They should flow naturally at the proper times. Your face should be expressive, not deadpan. Maintain eye contact with your audience. Watch your posture; stand straight at the podium.

3. Deliver a positive message; don't tear down. Don't be too tough against other causes.

4. Deliver a message you believe in: make it a personal message.

5. Paint a picture. Tell a story to illustrate your point.

6. Use change of pace in your voice and speed of delivery.

7. Use reiteration; repeat words. Use alliteration, a string of words starting with the same first letter or sound.

8. Synonyms add to the picture; use antonyms – opposites - for effect and to express extremes.

9. Use a central theme to unite the whole message. Refer to the theme with a refrain.

10. Use rich, colorful language.

11. Use pepper and salt. Consider your main theme the steak you are serving, but use a few lively words or thoughts as seasoning.

12. Build to a conclusion and summarize at the end.

13. Don't memorize your speech word for word and don't read it. Know the first and last sentences by heart.

Appendix A

Openings with a Challenge

▸ Take a giant step...

▸ Do something extraordinary!

▸ Be a winner!

▸ Discover the...

▸ Explore the...

▸ Encounter the...

▸ Experience the...

▸ Meet the...

▸ Learn about the...

▸ Sample the...

▸ Relive the...

▸ Say yes to...

▸ Join the...

▸ Capture the...

▸ Cross the threshold...

▸ If you're seriously interested in...

▸ If you sincerely want to...

▸ Join the small handful of people who...

▸ ...like a professional!

- ▸ Match wits with...
- ▸ Make time for...
- ▸ Return to the...
- ▸ Delve into the...
- ▸ Visit the...
- ▸ Enjoy the...
- ▸ Let your imagination soar!
- ▸ Be your own...
- ▸ If you think you're good enough...

Appendix B

Openings with a Question

▸ Isn't it time you...?

▸ Did you know that...?

▸ Are you still...?

▸ Want to keep in touch with...?

▸ Want to stay abreast of...?

▸ Are you interested in...?

▸ Are you curious about...?

▸ Are you intrigued by...?

▸ Will you be ready for the...?

▸ Who could say no to...?

▸ Do you want a better job?

▸ Could you use an extra $____ each month?

▸ What's the best investment you could make?

▸ How secure is your job?

▸ Why postpone your future in...?

▸ What would you say if we offered to help you...?

▸ Have you ever stayed awake at night thinking about...?

▸ How many times have you said to yourself _____?

- Did you ever ask yourself...?
- Don't you need...?
- Don't you wish...?
- Wouldn't you like to...?
- Confused about which _____ to buy?
- Why should you use _____ when you can...?
- Tired of the same old _____?
- Why trade a _____ for a _____?
- Why sacrifice _____ for _____?
- Who can put a price on _____?
- Are you ready for...?
- Do you want to stretch your purchasing power?
- Have you ever thought about...?
- What's the most effective way to...?
- What's the most profitable...?
- What's the safest...?

Appendix C

Openings with a Statement

▸ It's no secret that...

▸ We'll change you mind about...

▸ You've probably noticed that...

▸ Just wait until you...

▸ The results are in.

▸ It's not every day that...

▸ Forget everything you've heard about...

▸ Don't let _____ keep you from getting ahead.

▸ _____ often spells the difference between failure and success.

▸ Within 30 days from today, you could be...

▸ You can organize a successful _____.

▸ Think about...

▸ Now you can...

▸ For under $_____ you can...

▸ You're the kind of person who...

▸ Believe it or not...

▸ You're in for a pleasant surprise.

▸ If you're like most people, you probably...

- If _____ is your passion, then you'll appreciate…
- In today's competitive marketplace…
- In today's uncertain economy,…
- We live in an increasingly _____ society.
- Today, more than ever…
- It's a fact of life that…
- It's never too early to…
- It's never too late to…
- Now, the real truth about…
- Your new career in _____ is just weeks away.
- Anyone who knows _____ will tell you that…
- It isn't enough to be…
- Every once in a while you come across a _____ that may determine the future of…
- If you're been waiting for the right _____, you don't have to wait any longer.
- It's hard enough to _____ without having to worry about _____.
- Let's be honest.
- Let's face it.
- If you'd like to become part of today's _____, there's no better way to start than…